THE LEGEND OF KORRA

Created by
BRYAN KONIETZKO
MICHAEL DANTE DiMARTINO

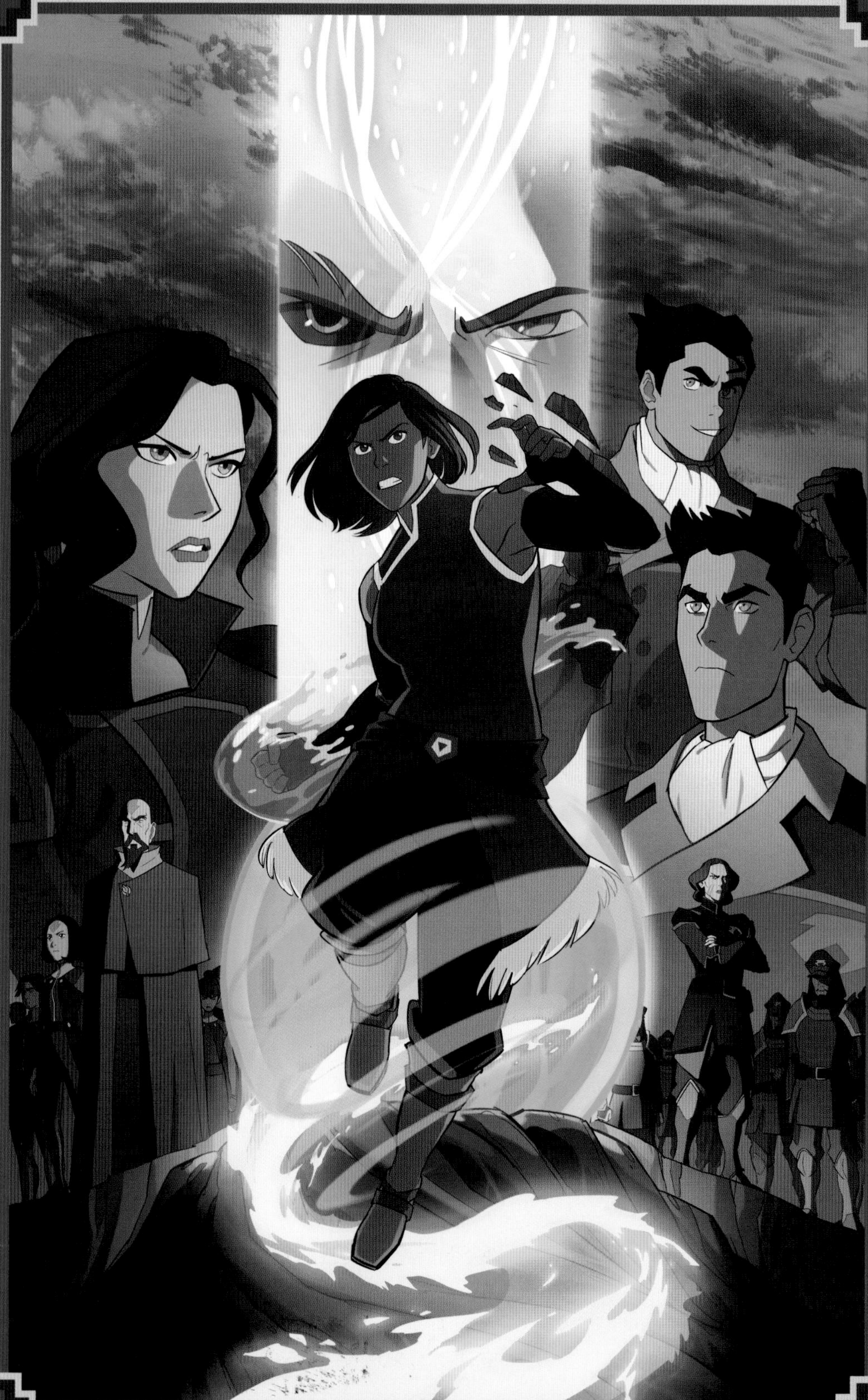

THE LEGEND OF KORRA

TURF WARS · PART THREE

written by
MICHAEL DANTE DiMARTINO

layouts by
IRENE KOH and **PAUL REINWAND**

art by
IRENE KOH

colors by
VIVIAN NG

color assistance by
MARISSA LOUISE

lettering by
NATE PIEKOS of Blambot®

cover by
HEATHER CAMPBELL with **VIVIAN NG**

DARK HORSE BOOKS

president and publisher **MIKE RICHARDSON**

editor **DAVE MARSHALL**   assistant editor **RACHEL ROBERTS**

designer **SARAH TERRY**   digital art technician **CHRISTIANNE GOUDREAU**

Special thanks to Linda Lee, Kat van Dam, James Salerno, and Joan Hilty
at Nickelodeon, and to Bryan Konietzko and Michael Dante DiMartino.

Published by **DARK HORSE BOOKS**
A division of Dark Horse Comics, Inc.
10956 SE Main Street, Milwaukie, OR 97222

DARKHORSE.COM | **NICK.COM**

International Licensing: (503) 905-2377
Comic Shop Locator Service: comicshoplocator.com

First edition: June 2018 | ISBN 978-1-50670-185-1

1 3 5 7 9 10 8 6 4 2
Printed in China

Neil Hankerson Executive Vice President • **Tom Weddle** Chief Financial Officer • **Randy Stradley** Vice
President of Publishing • **Nick McWhorter** Chief Business Development Officer • **Matt Parkinson** Vice
President of Marketing • **Dale LaFountain** Vice President of Information Technology • **Cara Niece** Vice
President of Production and Scheduling • **Mark Bernardi** Vice President of Book Trade and Digital Sales
• **Ken Lizzi** General Counsel • **Dave Marshall** Editor in Chief • **Davey Estrada** Editorial Director • **Chris
Warner** Senior Books Editor • **Cary Grazzini** Director of Specialty Projects • **Lia Ribacchi** Art Director •
Vanessa Todd Director of Print Purchasing • **Matt Dryer** Director of Digital Art and Prepress • **Michael
Gombos** Director of International Publishing and Licensing • **Kari Yadro** Director of Custom Programs

Library of Congress Cataloging-in-Publication Data

Names: DiMartino, Michael Dante, author. | Koh, Irene (Comic book artist),
   artist. | Ng, Vivian, colourist. | Piekos, Nate, letterer.
Title: The Legend of Korra : turf wars / written by Michael Dante DiMartino ;
   art by Irene Koh.
Other titles: Legend of Korra (Television program)
Description: First edition. | Milwaukie, OR : Dark Horse Books, 2017- | Part
   one: colors by Vivian Ng ; lettering by Nate Piekos of Blambot ; cover by
   Heather Campbell with Jane Bak.
Identifiers: LCCN 2017015317 | ISBN 9781506700151 (part one : paperback)
Subjects: LCSH: Comic books, strips, etc. | BISAC: COMICS & GRAPHIC NOVELS /
   Media Tie-In.
Classification: LCC PN6728.L434 D56 2017 | DDC 741.5/973--dc23
LC record available at https://lccn.loc.gov/2017015317

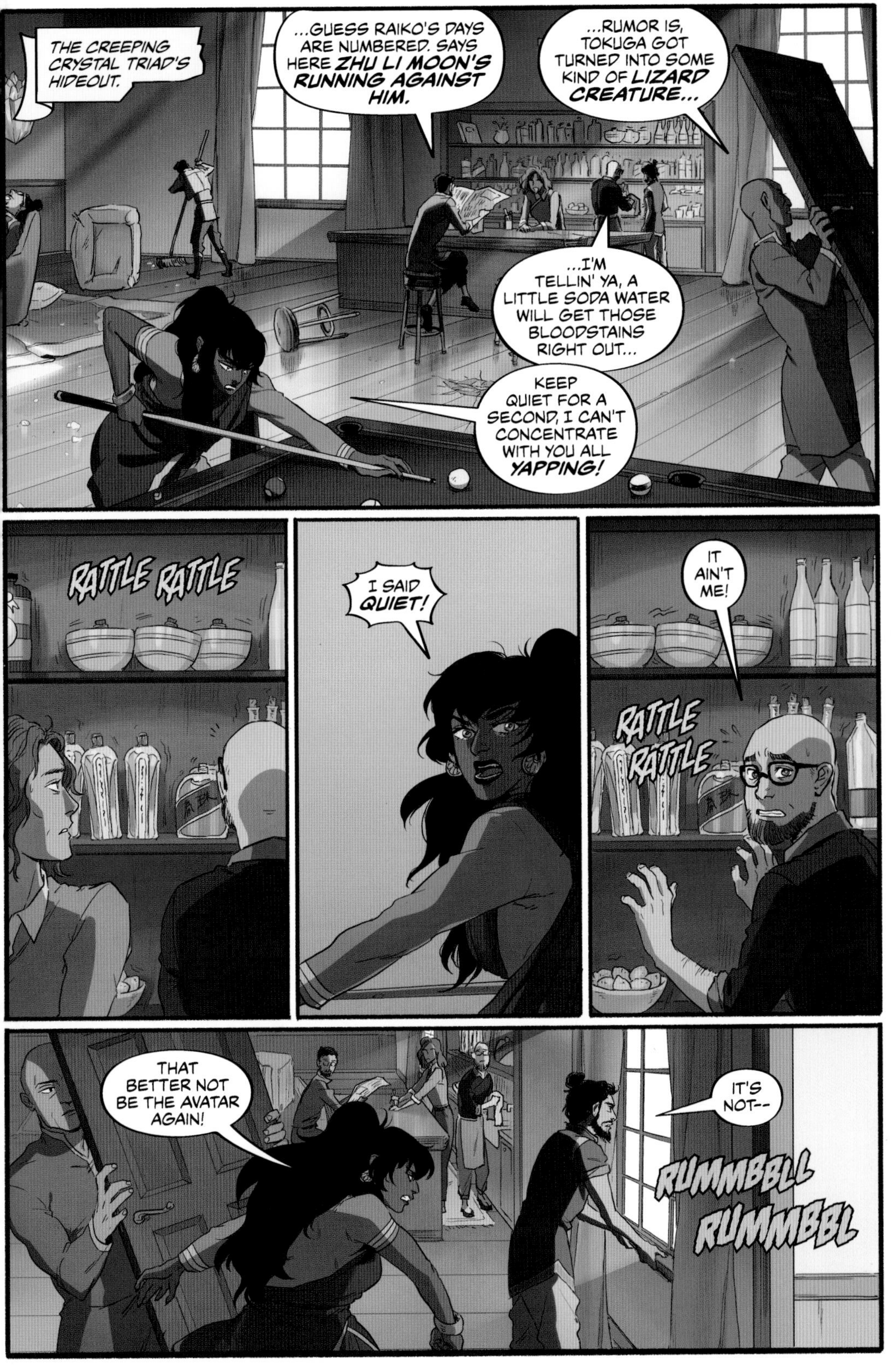
THE CREEPING CRYSTAL TRIAD'S HIDEOUT.
...GUESS RAIKO'S DAYS ARE NUMBERED. SAYS HERE ZHU LI MOON'S RUNNING AGAINST HIM.
...RUMOR IS, TOKUGA GOT TURNED INTO SOME KIND OF LIZARD CREATURE...
...I'M TELLIN' YA, A LITTLE SODA WATER WILL GET THOSE BLOODSTAINS RIGHT OUT...
KEEP QUIET FOR A SECOND, I CAN'T CONCENTRATE WITH YOU ALL YAPPING!
RATTLE RATTLE
I SAID QUIET!
IT AIN'T ME!
RATTLE RATTLE
THAT BETTER NOT BE THE AVATAR AGAIN!
IT'S NOT--
RUMMBBLL RUMMBBL

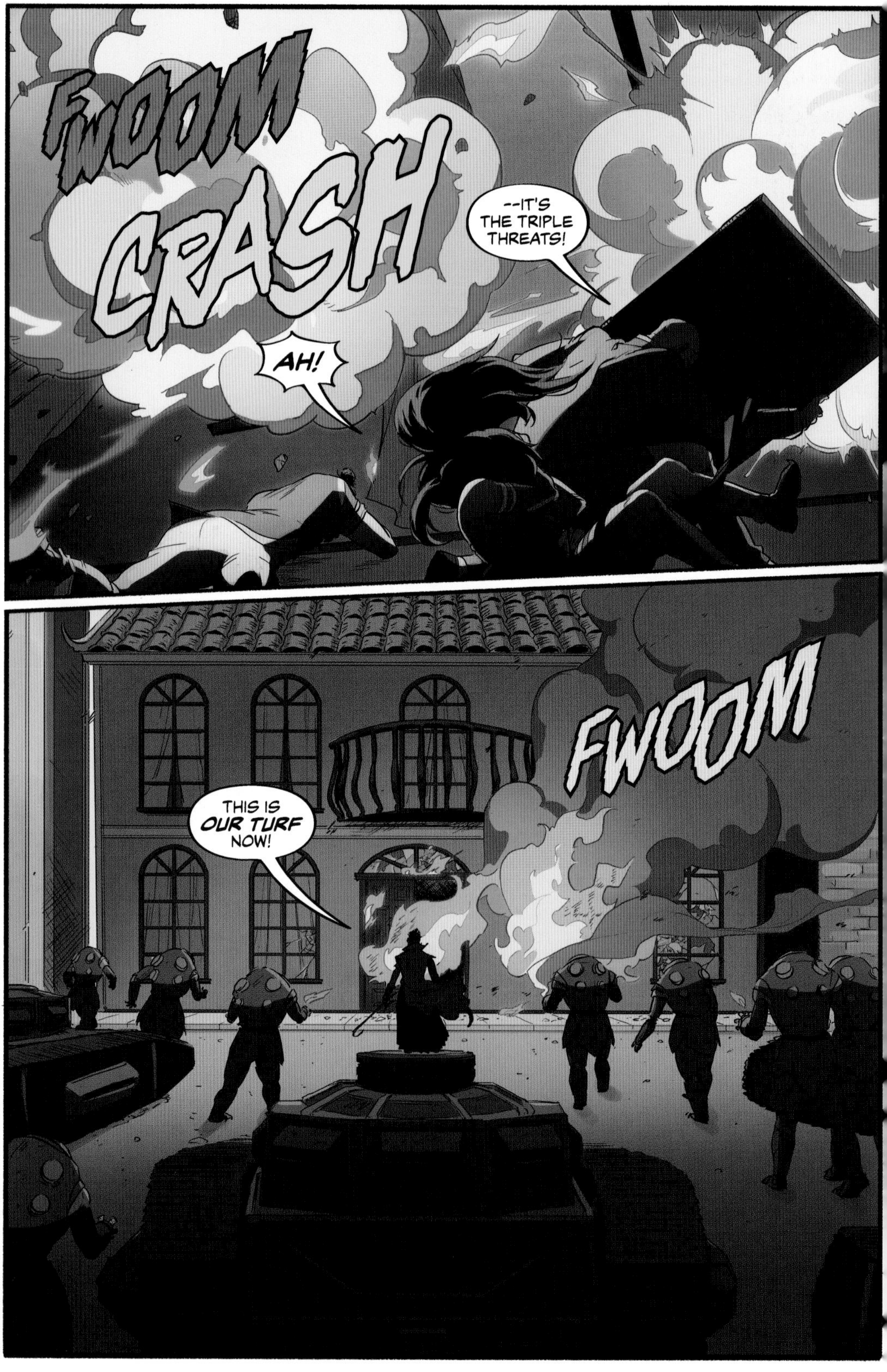
FWOOM
CRASH
--IT'S THE TRIPLE THREATS!
AH!
FWOOM
THIS IS OUR TURF NOW!

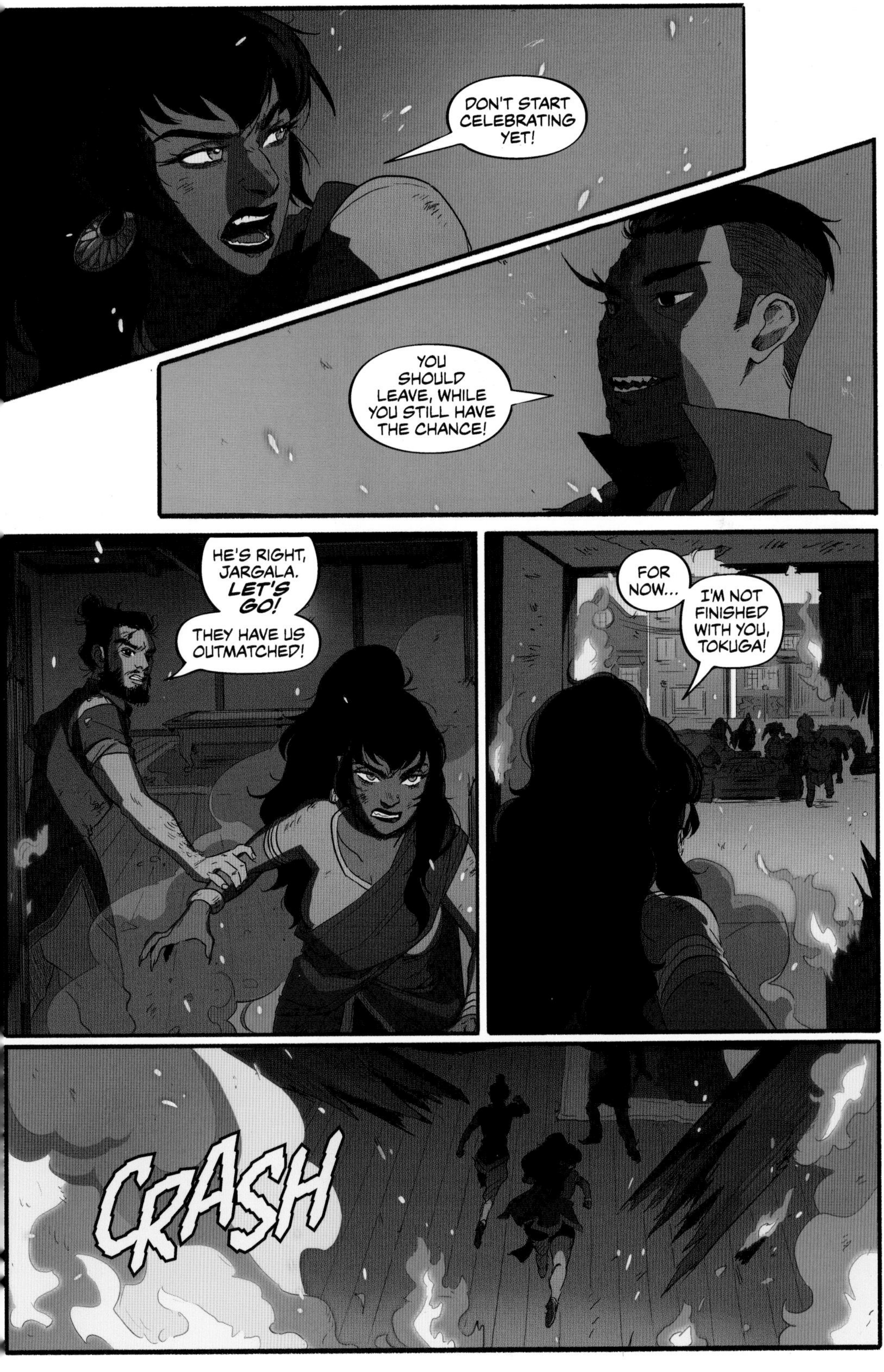
DON'T START CELEBRATING YET!
YOU SHOULD LEAVE, WHILE YOU STILL HAVE THE CHANCE!
HE'S RIGHT, JARGALA. **LET'S GO!**
THEY HAVE US OUTMATCHED!
FOR NOW...
I'M NOT FINISHED WITH YOU, TOKUGA!
CRASH

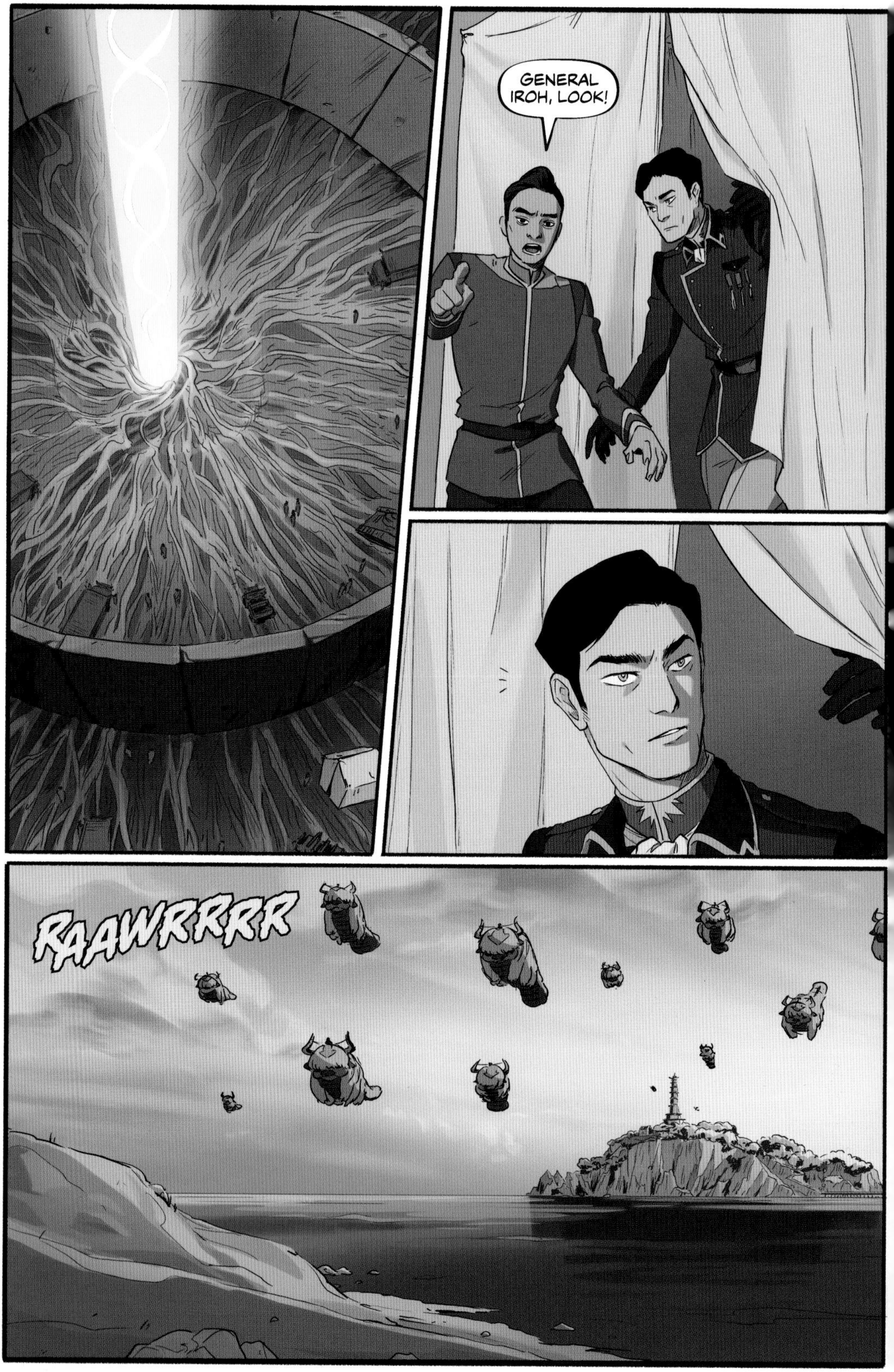
GENERAL IROH, LOOK!
RAAWRRRR

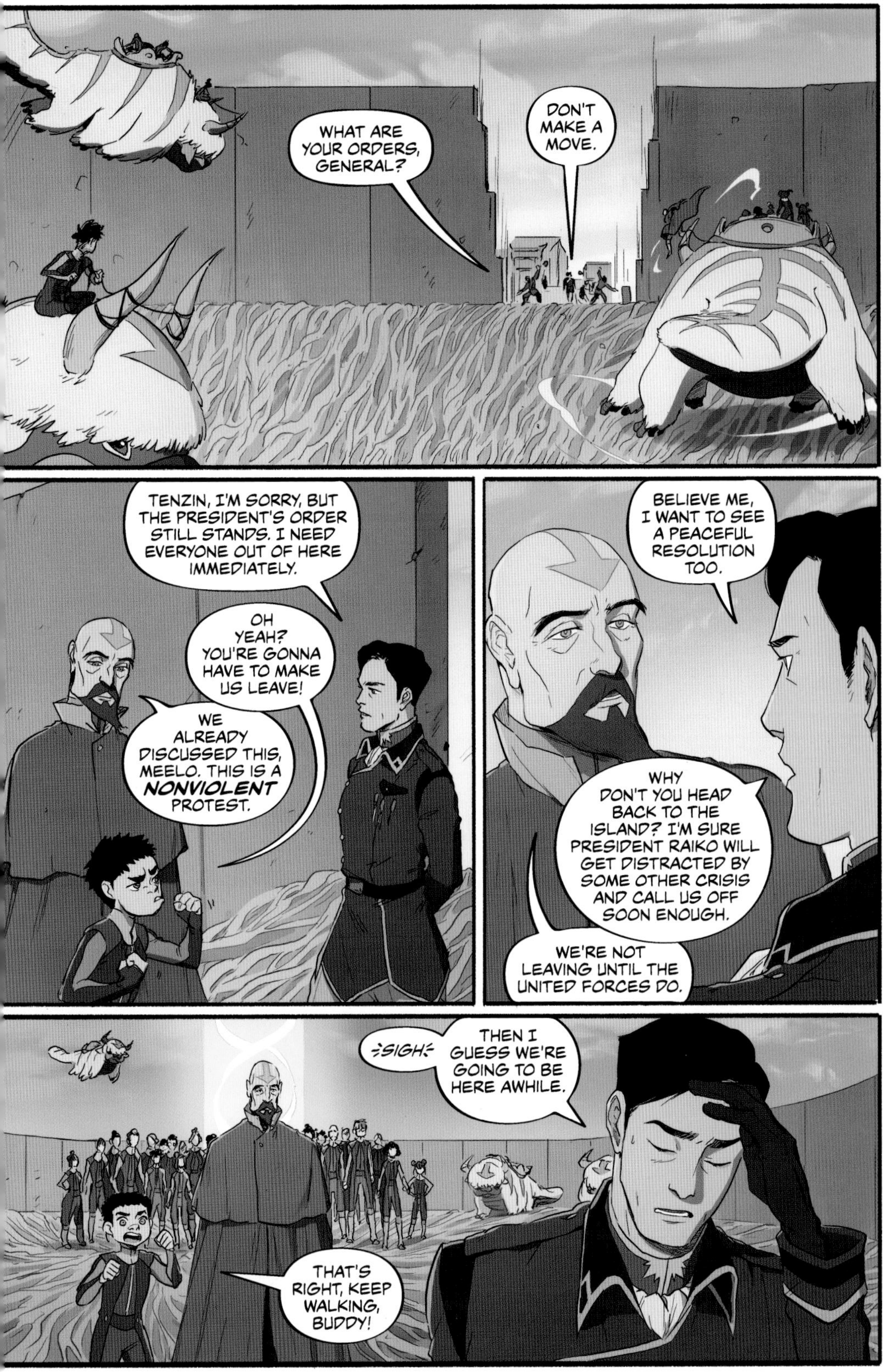

WHAT ARE YOUR ORDERS, GENERAL?
DON'T MAKE A MOVE.
TENZIN, I'M SORRY, BUT THE PRESIDENT'S ORDER STILL STANDS. I NEED EVERYONE OUT OF HERE IMMEDIATELY.
OH YEAH? YOU'RE GONNA HAVE TO MAKE US LEAVE!
WE ALREADY DISCUSSED THIS, MEELO. THIS IS A **NONVIOLENT** PROTEST.
BELIEVE ME, I WANT TO SEE A PEACEFUL RESOLUTION TOO.
WHY DON'T YOU HEAD BACK TO THE ISLAND? I'M SURE PRESIDENT RAIKO WILL GET DISTRACTED BY SOME OTHER CRISIS AND CALL US OFF SOON ENOUGH.
WE'RE NOT LEAVING UNTIL THE UNITED FORCES DO.
SIGH
THEN I GUESS WE'RE GOING TO BE HERE AWHILE.
THAT'S RIGHT, KEEP WALKING, BUDDY!

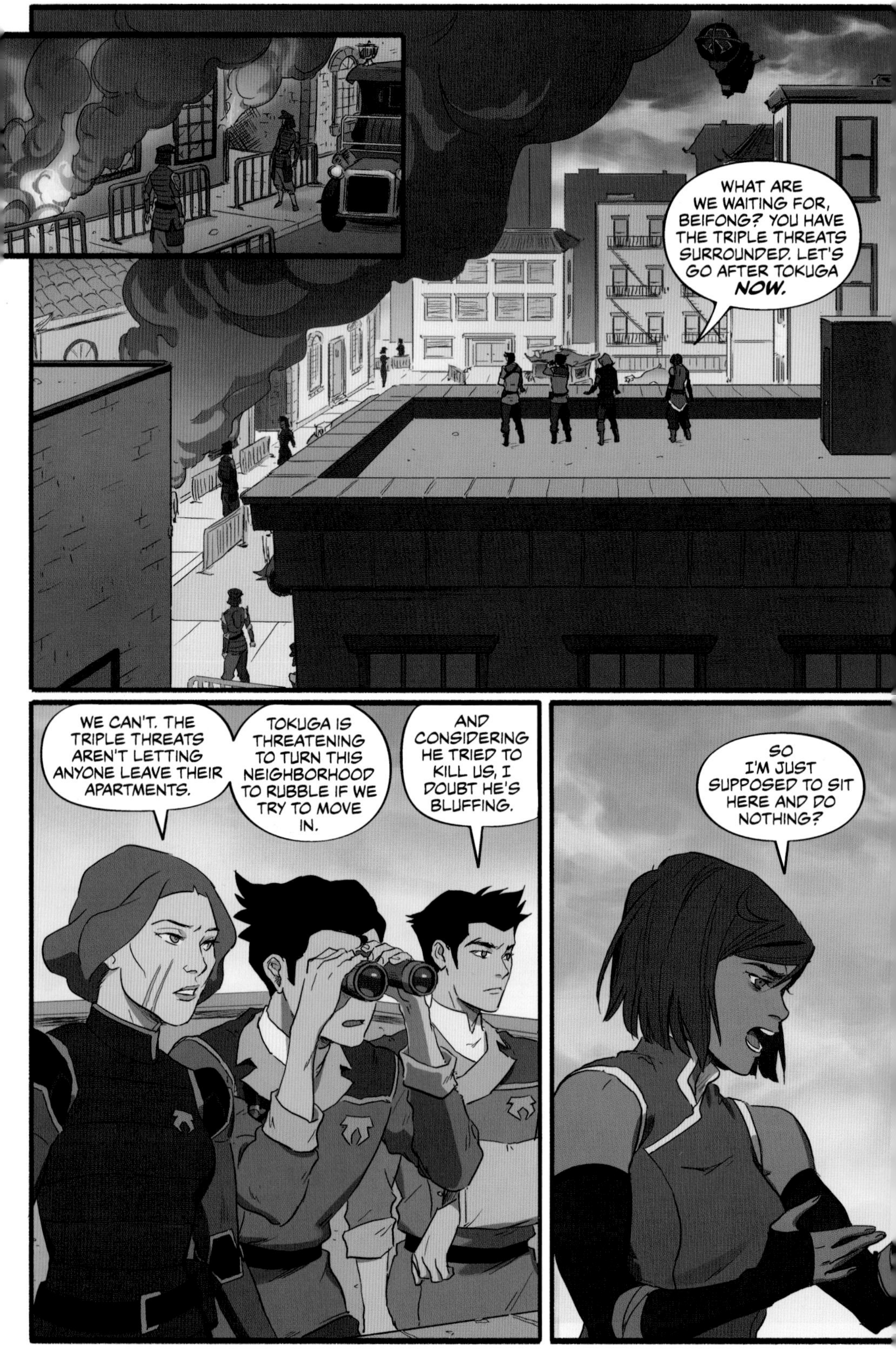
WHAT ARE WE WAITING FOR, BEIFONG? YOU HAVE THE TRIPLE THREATS SURROUNDED. LET'S GO AFTER TOKUGA *NOW.*
WE CAN'T. THE TRIPLE THREATS AREN'T LETTING ANYONE LEAVE THEIR APARTMENTS.
TOKUGA IS THREATENING TO TURN THIS NEIGHBORHOOD TO RUBBLE IF WE TRY TO MOVE IN.
AND CONSIDERING HE TRIED TO KILL US, I DOUBT HE'S BLUFFING.
SO I'M JUST SUPPOSED TO SIT HERE AND DO NOTHING?

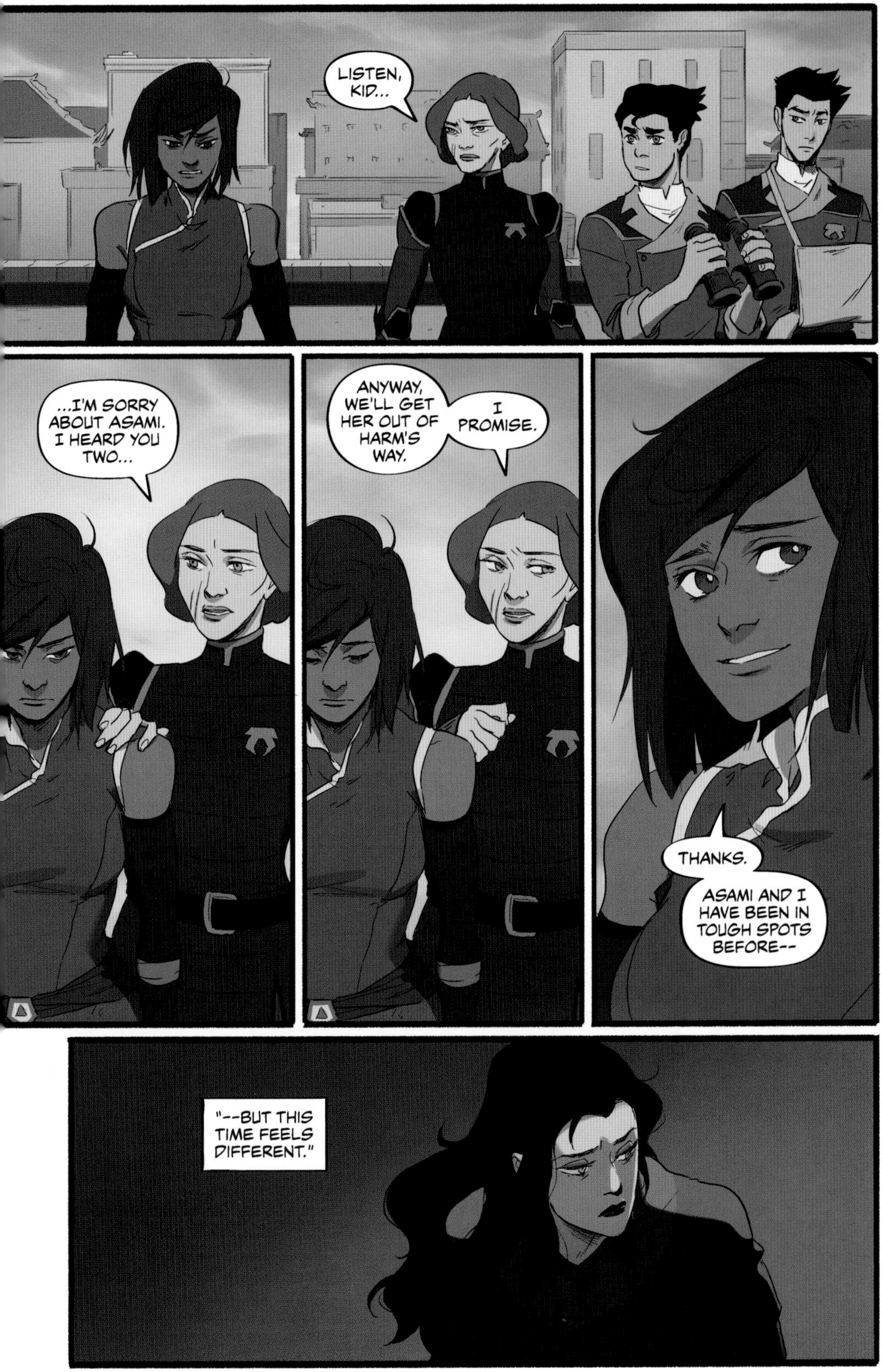
LISTEN, KID...
...I'M SORRY ABOUT ASAMI. I HEARD YOU TWO...
ANYWAY, WE'LL GET HER OUT OF HARM'S WAY.
I PROMISE.
THANKS.
ASAMI AND I HAVE BEEN IN TOUGH SPOTS BEFORE--
"--BUT THIS TIME FEELS DIFFERENT."

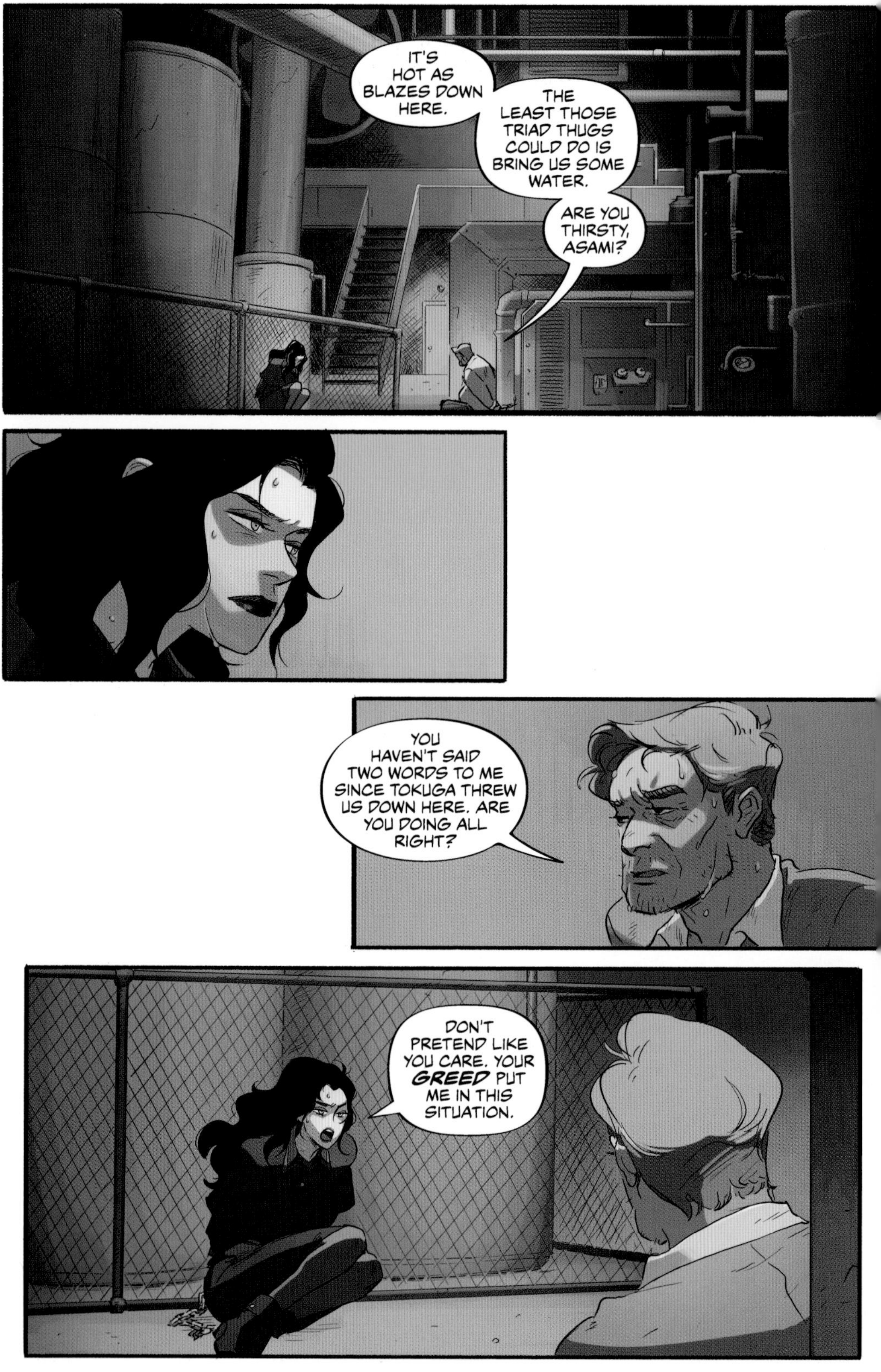
IT'S HOT AS BLAZES DOWN HERE.
THE LEAST THOSE TRIAD THUGS COULD DO IS BRING US SOME WATER.
ARE YOU THIRSTY, ASAMI?
YOU HAVEN'T SAID TWO WORDS TO ME SINCE TOKUGA THREW US DOWN HERE. ARE YOU DOING ALL RIGHT?
DON'T PRETEND LIKE YOU CARE. YOUR GREED PUT ME IN THIS SITUATION.

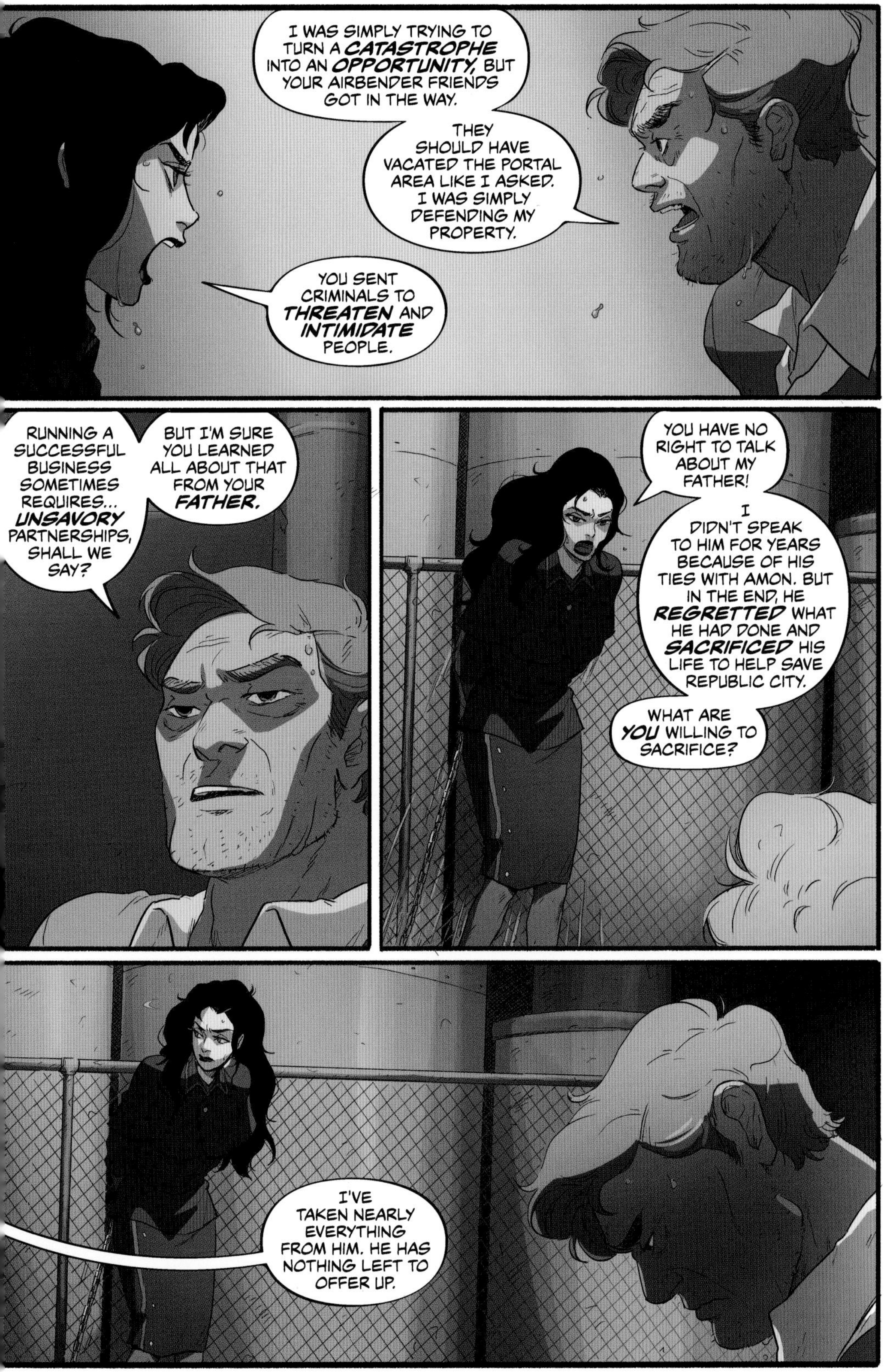
I WAS SIMPLY TRYING TO TURN A CATASTROPHE INTO AN OPPORTUNITY, BUT YOUR AIRBENDER FRIENDS GOT IN THE WAY.
THEY SHOULD HAVE VACATED THE PORTAL AREA LIKE I ASKED. I WAS SIMPLY DEFENDING MY PROPERTY.
YOU SENT CRIMINALS TO THREATEN AND INTIMIDATE PEOPLE.
RUNNING A SUCCESSFUL BUSINESS SOMETIMES REQUIRES... UNSAVORY PARTNERSHIPS, SHALL WE SAY?
BUT I'M SURE YOU LEARNED ALL ABOUT THAT FROM YOUR FATHER.
YOU HAVE NO RIGHT TO TALK ABOUT MY FATHER!
I DIDN'T SPEAK TO HIM FOR YEARS BECAUSE OF HIS TIES WITH AMON. BUT IN THE END, HE REGRETTED WHAT HE HAD DONE AND SACRIFICED HIS LIFE TO HELP SAVE REPUBLIC CITY.
WHAT ARE YOU WILLING TO SACRIFICE?
I'VE TAKEN NEARLY EVERYTHING FROM HIM. HE HAS NOTHING LEFT TO OFFER UP.

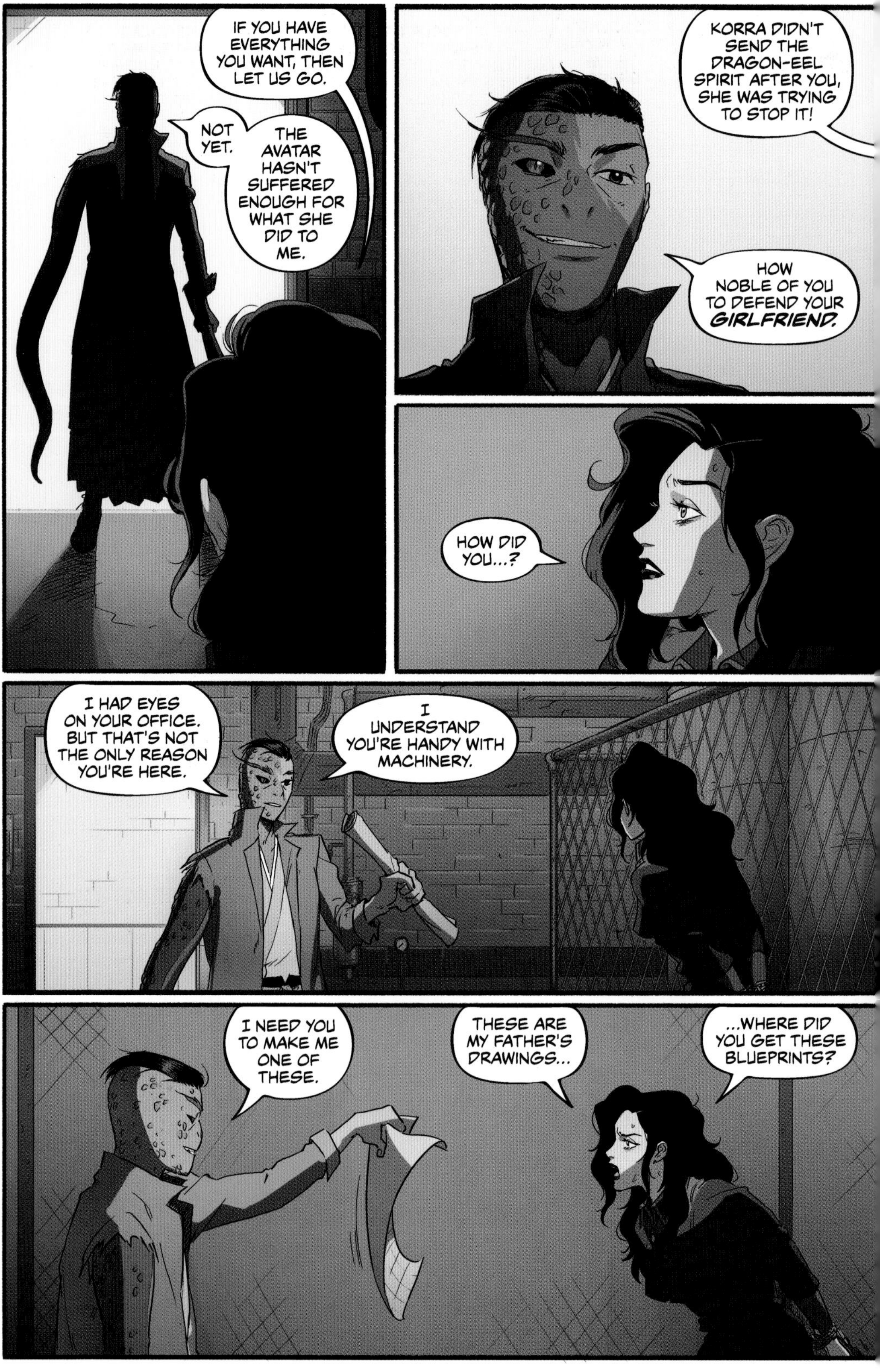
IF YOU HAVE EVERYTHING YOU WANT, THEN LET US GO.
NOT YET.
THE AVATAR HASN'T SUFFERED ENOUGH FOR WHAT SHE DID TO ME.
KORRA DIDN'T SEND THE DRAGON-EEL SPIRIT AFTER YOU, SHE WAS TRYING TO STOP IT!
HOW NOBLE OF YOU TO DEFEND YOUR GIRLFRIEND.
HOW DID YOU...?
I HAD EYES ON YOUR OFFICE. BUT THAT'S NOT THE ONLY REASON YOU'RE HERE.
I UNDERSTAND YOU'RE HANDY WITH MACHINERY.
I NEED YOU TO MAKE ME ONE OF THESE.
THESE ARE MY FATHER'S DRAWINGS...
...WHERE DID YOU GET THESE BLUEPRINTS?

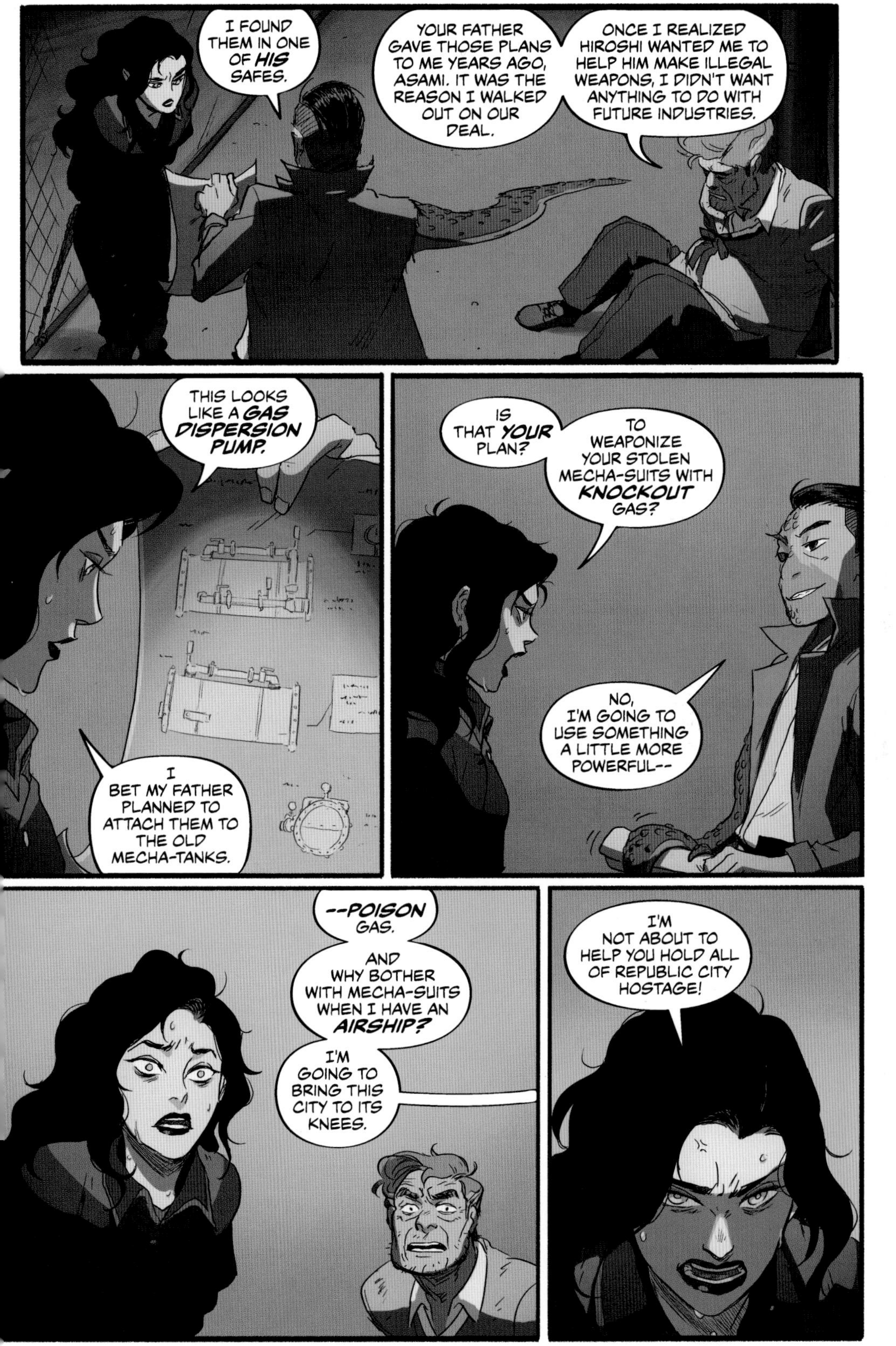

I FOUND THEM IN ONE OF HIS SAFES.
YOUR FATHER GAVE THOSE PLANS TO ME YEARS AGO, ASAMI. IT WAS THE REASON I WALKED OUT ON OUR DEAL.
ONCE I REALIZED HIROSHI WANTED ME TO HELP HIM MAKE ILLEGAL WEAPONS, I DIDN'T WANT ANYTHING TO DO WITH FUTURE INDUSTRIES.
THIS LOOKS LIKE A GAS DISPERSION PUMP.
I BET MY FATHER PLANNED TO ATTACH THEM TO THE OLD MECHA-TANKS.
IS THAT YOUR PLAN?
TO WEAPONIZE YOUR STOLEN MECHA-SUITS WITH KNOCKOUT GAS?
NO, I'M GOING TO USE SOMETHING A LITTLE MORE POWERFUL--
--POISON GAS.
AND WHY BOTHER WITH MECHA-SUITS WHEN I HAVE AN AIRSHIP?
I'M GOING TO BRING THIS CITY TO ITS KNEES.
I'M NOT ABOUT TO HELP YOU HOLD ALL OF REPUBLIC CITY HOSTAGE!

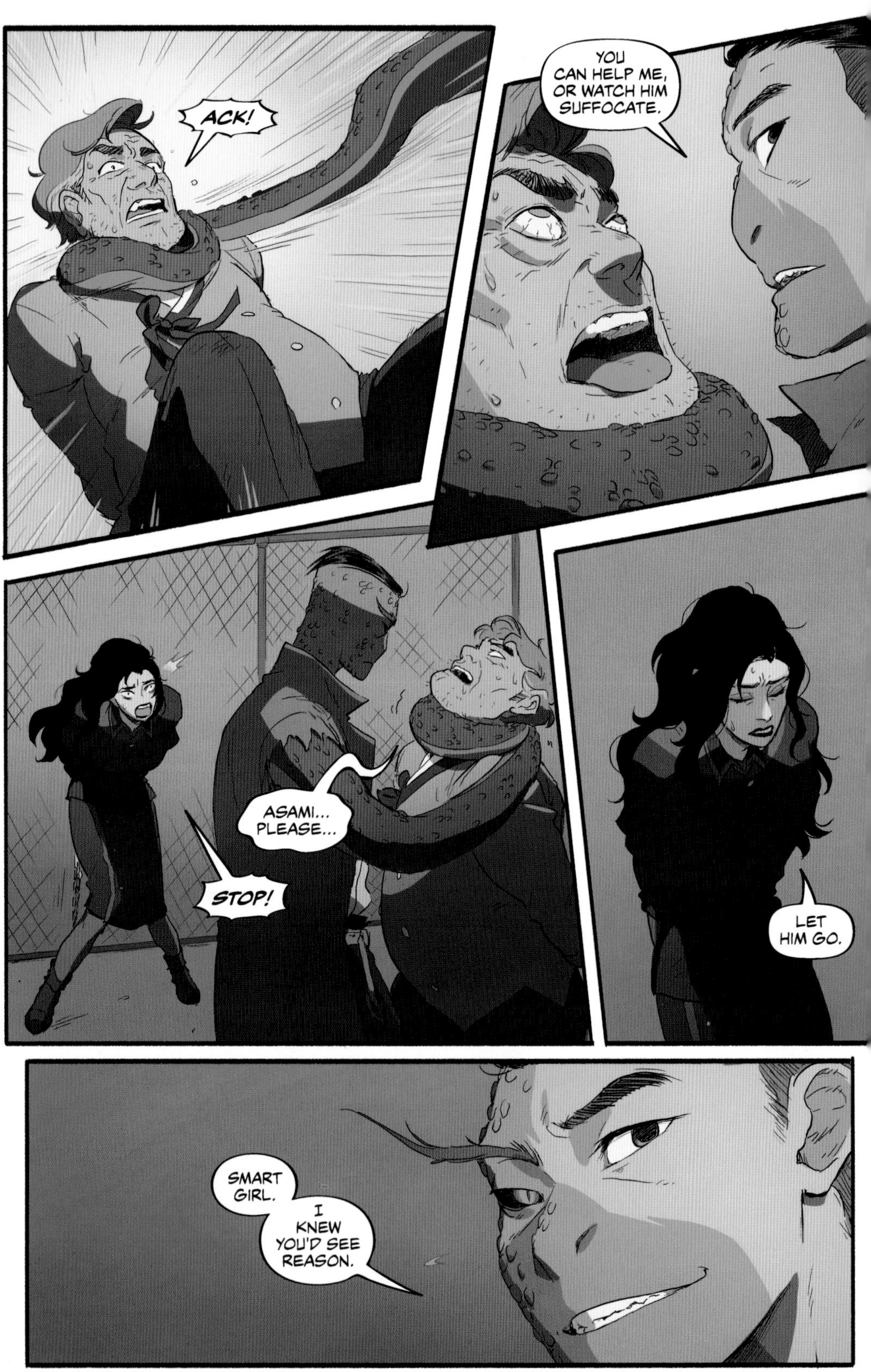
ACK!
YOU CAN HELP ME, OR WATCH HIM SUFFOCATE.
STOP!
ASAMI... PLEASE...
LET HIM GO.
SMART GIRL.
I KNEW YOU'D SEE REASON.

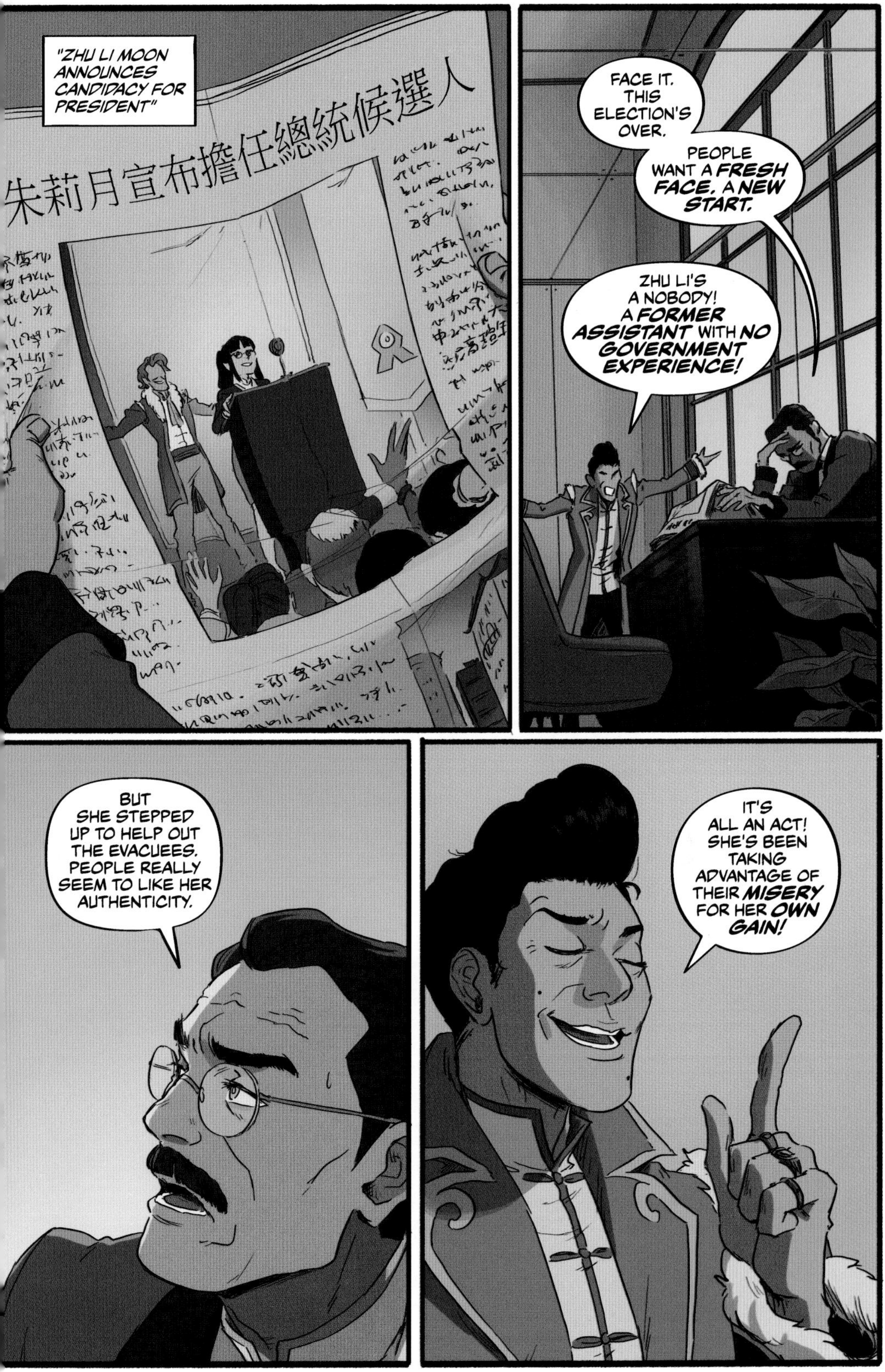
"ZHU LI MOON ANNOUNCES CANDIDACY FOR PRESIDENT"
朱莉月宣布擔任總統候選人
FACE IT. THIS ELECTION'S OVER.
PEOPLE WANT A FRESH FACE, A NEW START.
ZHU LI'S A NOBODY! A FORMER ASSISTANT WITH NO GOVERNMENT EXPERIENCE!
BUT SHE STEPPED UP TO HELP OUT THE EVACUEES. PEOPLE REALLY SEEM TO LIKE HER AUTHENTICITY.
IT'S ALL AN ACT! SHE'S BEEN TAKING ADVANTAGE OF THEIR MISERY FOR HER OWN GAIN!

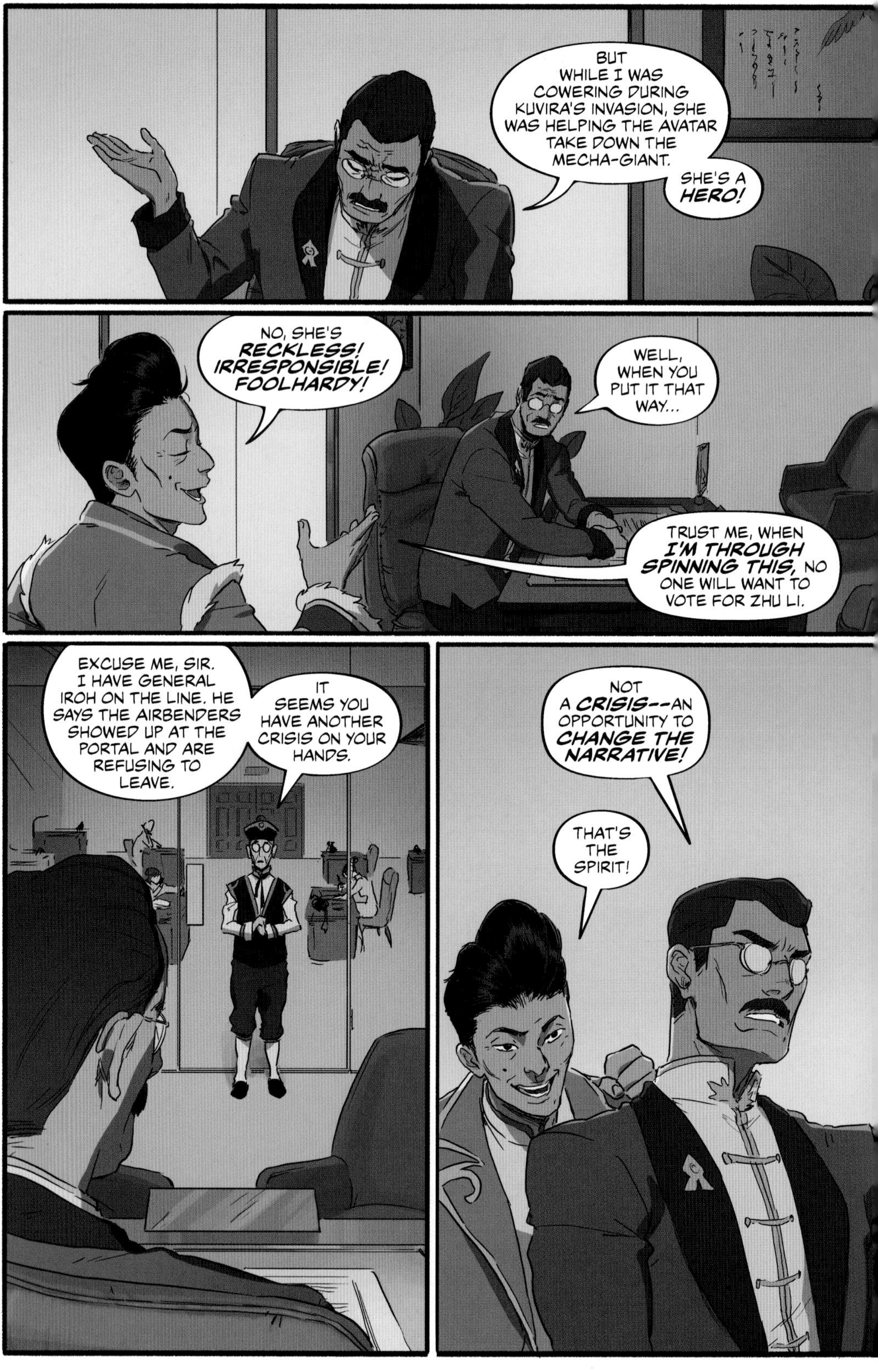
BUT WHILE I WAS COWERING DURING KUVIRA'S INVASION, SHE WAS HELPING THE AVATAR TAKE DOWN THE MECHA-GIANT.
SHE'S A HERO!
NO, SHE'S RECKLESS! IRRESPONSIBLE! FOOLHARDY!
WELL, WHEN YOU PUT IT THAT WAY...
TRUST ME, WHEN I'M THROUGH SPINNING THIS, NO ONE WILL WANT TO VOTE FOR ZHU LI.
EXCUSE ME, SIR. I HAVE GENERAL IROH ON THE LINE. HE SAYS THE AIRBENDERS SHOWED UP AT THE PORTAL AND ARE REFUSING TO LEAVE.
IT SEEMS YOU HAVE ANOTHER CRISIS ON YOUR HANDS.
NOT A CRISIS--AN OPPORTUNITY TO CHANGE THE NARRATIVE!
THAT'S THE SPIRIT!

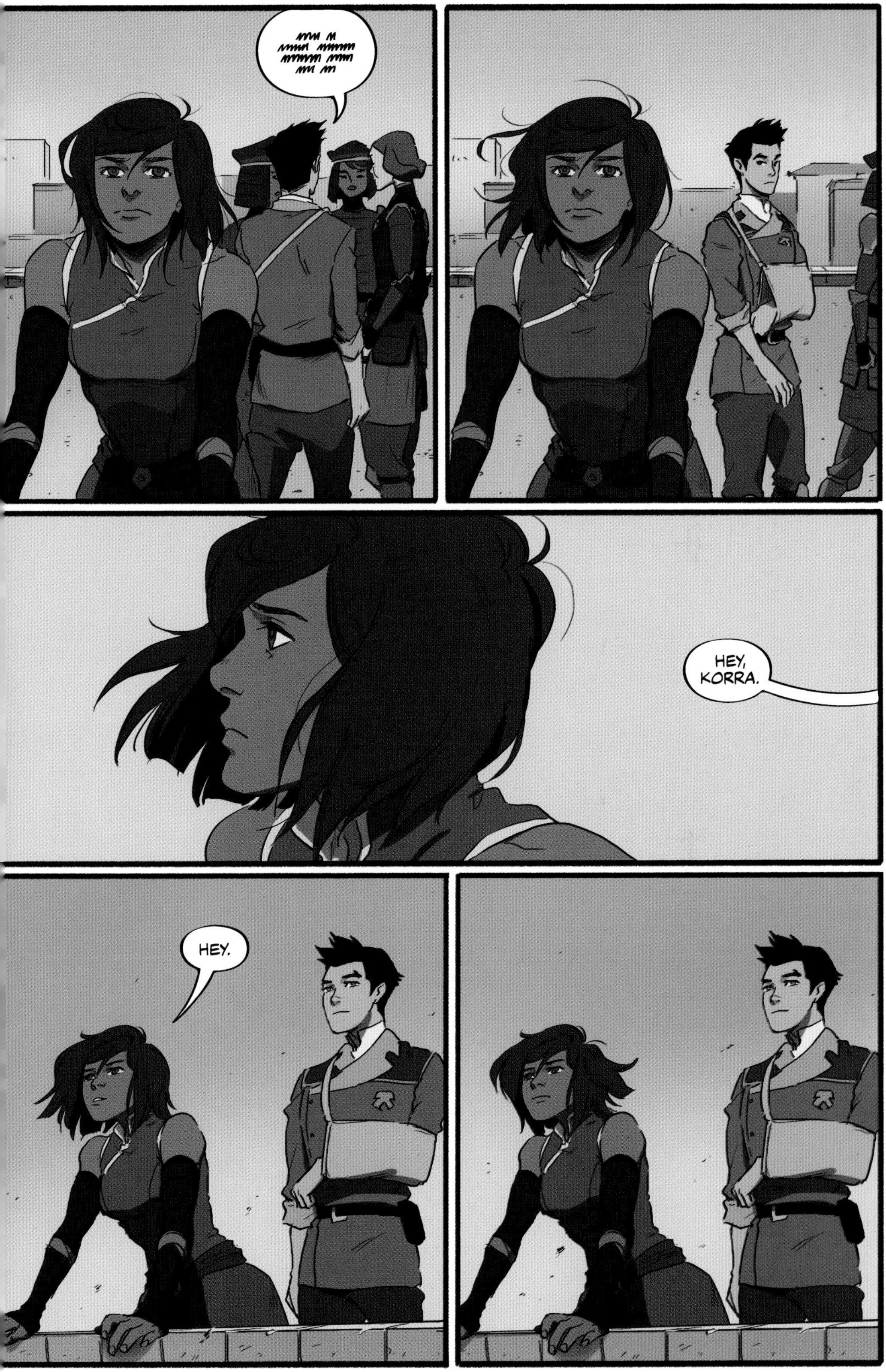
HEY, KORRA.
HEY.

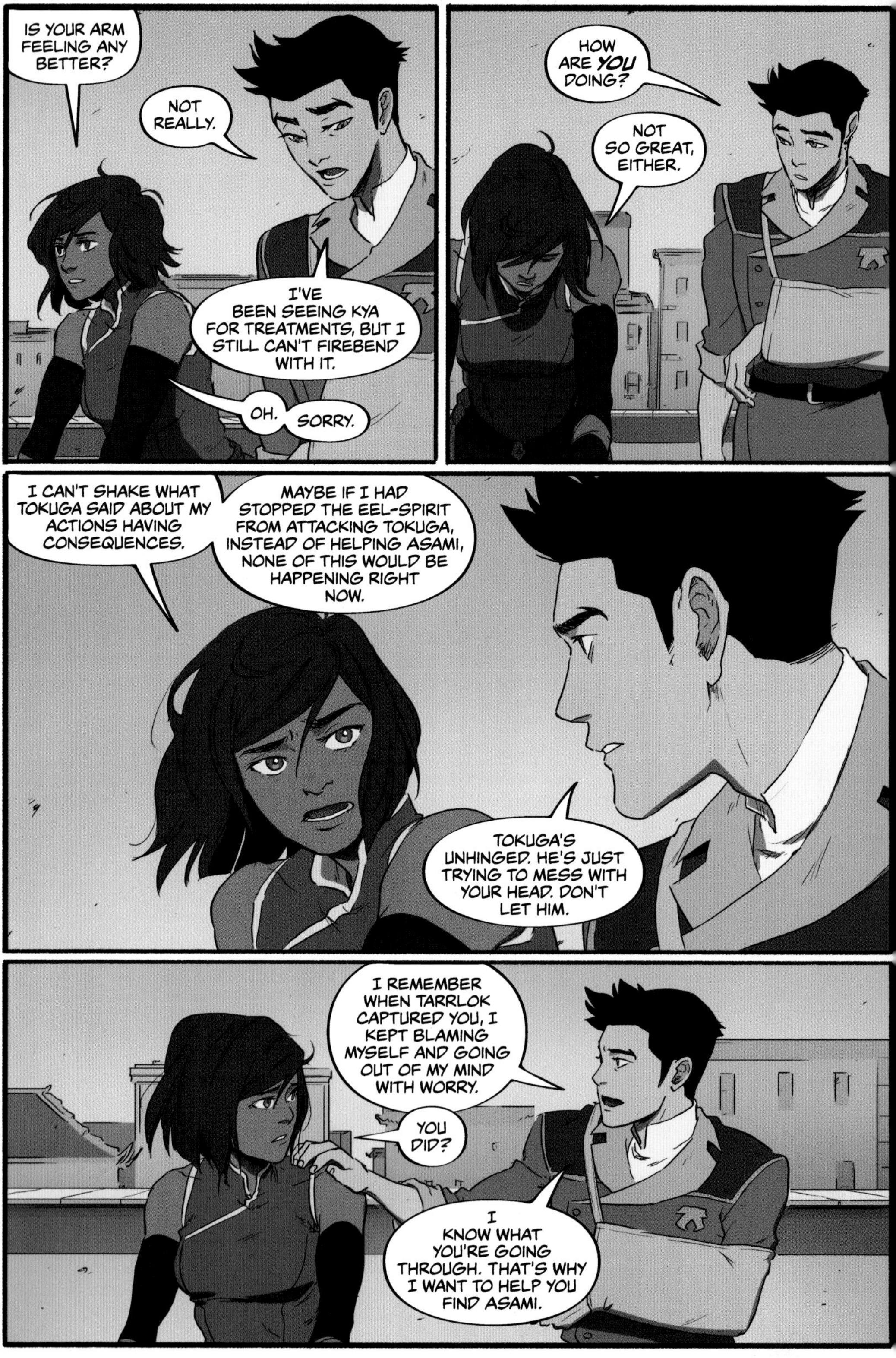
IS YOUR ARM FEELING ANY BETTER?
NOT REALLY.
I'VE BEEN SEEING KYA FOR TREATMENTS, BUT I STILL CAN'T FIREBEND WITH IT.
OH.
SORRY.
HOW ARE YOU DOING?
NOT SO GREAT, EITHER.
I CAN'T SHAKE WHAT TOKUGA SAID ABOUT MY ACTIONS HAVING CONSEQUENCES.
MAYBE IF I HAD STOPPED THE EEL-SPIRIT FROM ATTACKING TOKUGA, INSTEAD OF HELPING ASAMI, NONE OF THIS WOULD BE HAPPENING RIGHT NOW.
TOKUGA'S UNHINGED. HE'S JUST TRYING TO MESS WITH YOUR HEAD. DON'T LET HIM.
I REMEMBER WHEN TARRLOK CAPTURED YOU, I KEPT BLAMING MYSELF AND GOING OUT OF MY MIND WITH WORRY.
YOU DID?
I KNOW WHAT YOU'RE GOING THROUGH. THAT'S WHY I WANT TO HELP YOU FIND ASAMI.

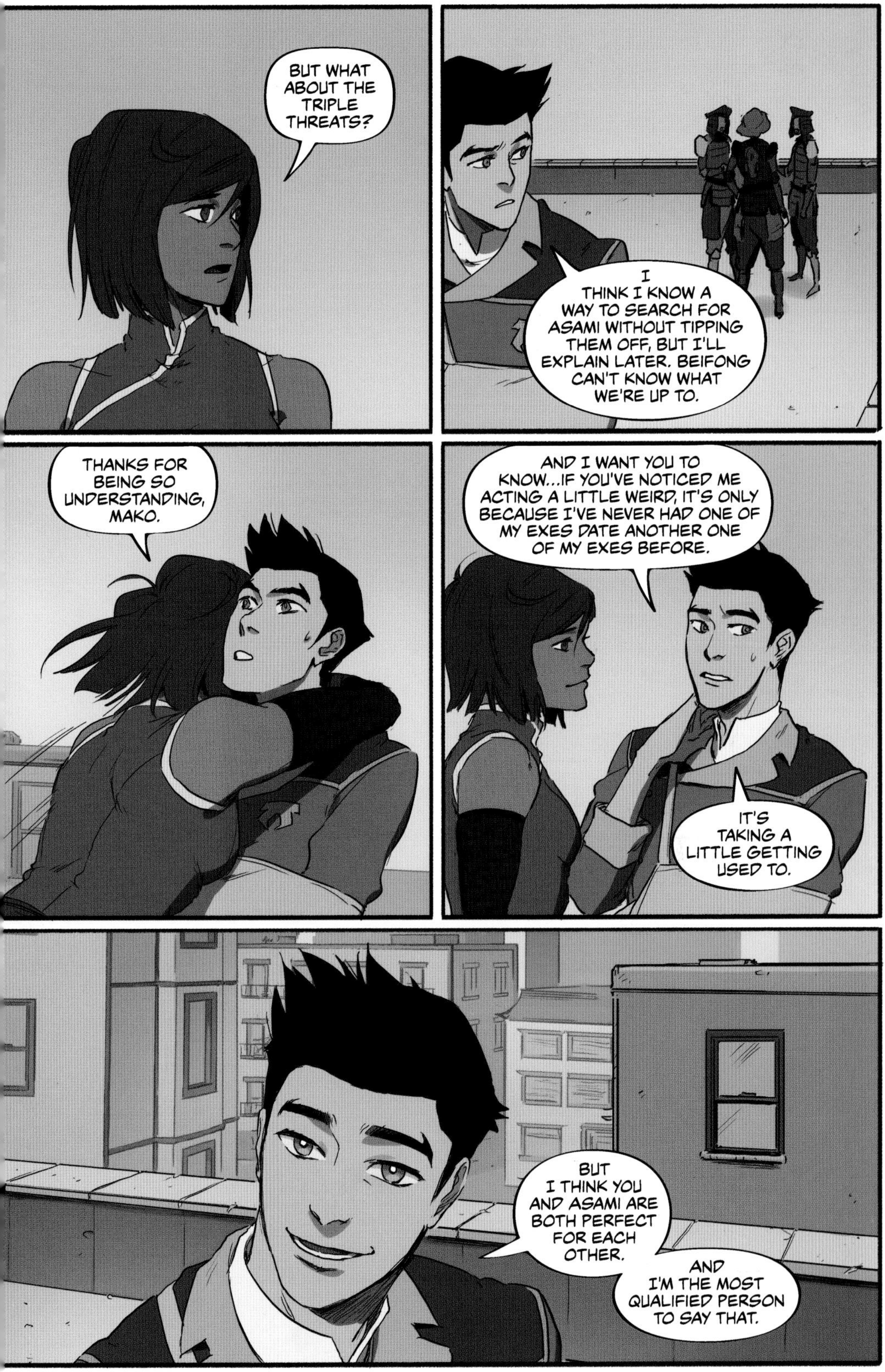
BUT WHAT ABOUT THE TRIPLE THREATS?
I THINK I KNOW A WAY TO SEARCH FOR ASAMI WITHOUT TIPPING THEM OFF, BUT I'LL EXPLAIN LATER. BEIFONG CAN'T KNOW WHAT WE'RE UP TO.
THANKS FOR BEING SO UNDERSTANDING, MAKO.
AND I WANT YOU TO KNOW...IF YOU'VE NOTICED ME ACTING A LITTLE WEIRD, IT'S ONLY BECAUSE I'VE NEVER HAD ONE OF MY EXES DATE ANOTHER ONE OF MY EXES BEFORE.
IT'S TAKING A LITTLE GETTING USED TO.
BUT I THINK YOU AND ASAMI ARE BOTH PERFECT FOR EACH OTHER.
AND I'M THE MOST QUALIFIED PERSON TO SAY THAT.

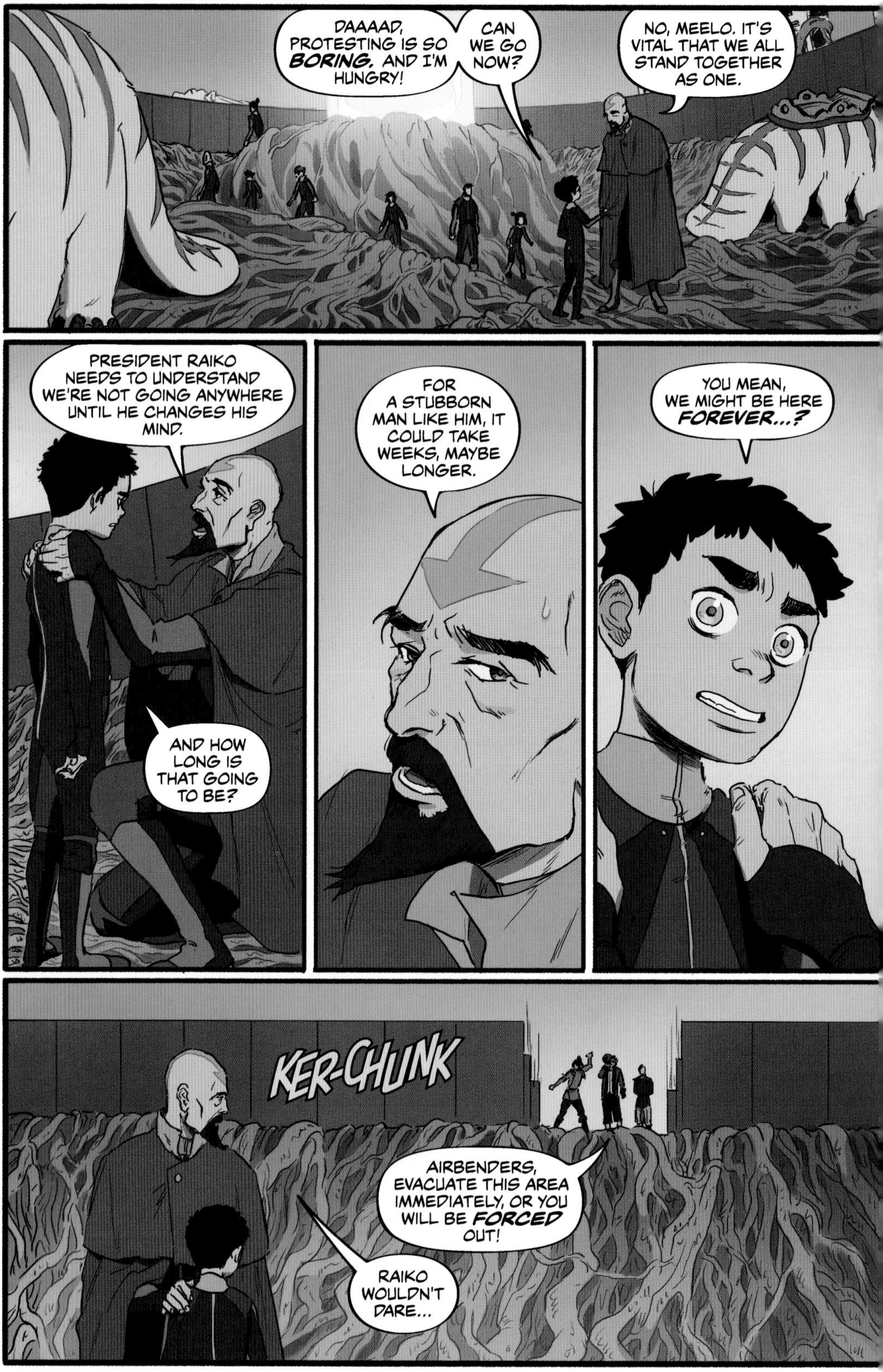
DAAAAD, PROTESTING IS SO BORING. AND I'M HUNGRY!
CAN WE GO NOW?
NO, MEELO. IT'S VITAL THAT WE ALL STAND TOGETHER AS ONE.
PRESIDENT RAIKO NEEDS TO UNDERSTAND WE'RE NOT GOING ANYWHERE UNTIL HE CHANGES HIS MIND.
AND HOW LONG IS THAT GOING TO BE?
FOR A STUBBORN MAN LIKE HIM, IT COULD TAKE WEEKS, MAYBE LONGER.
YOU MEAN, WE MIGHT BE HERE FOREVER...?
KER-CHUNK
AIRBENDERS, EVACUATE THIS AREA IMMEDIATELY, OR YOU WILL BE FORCED OUT!
RAIKO WOULDN'T DARE...

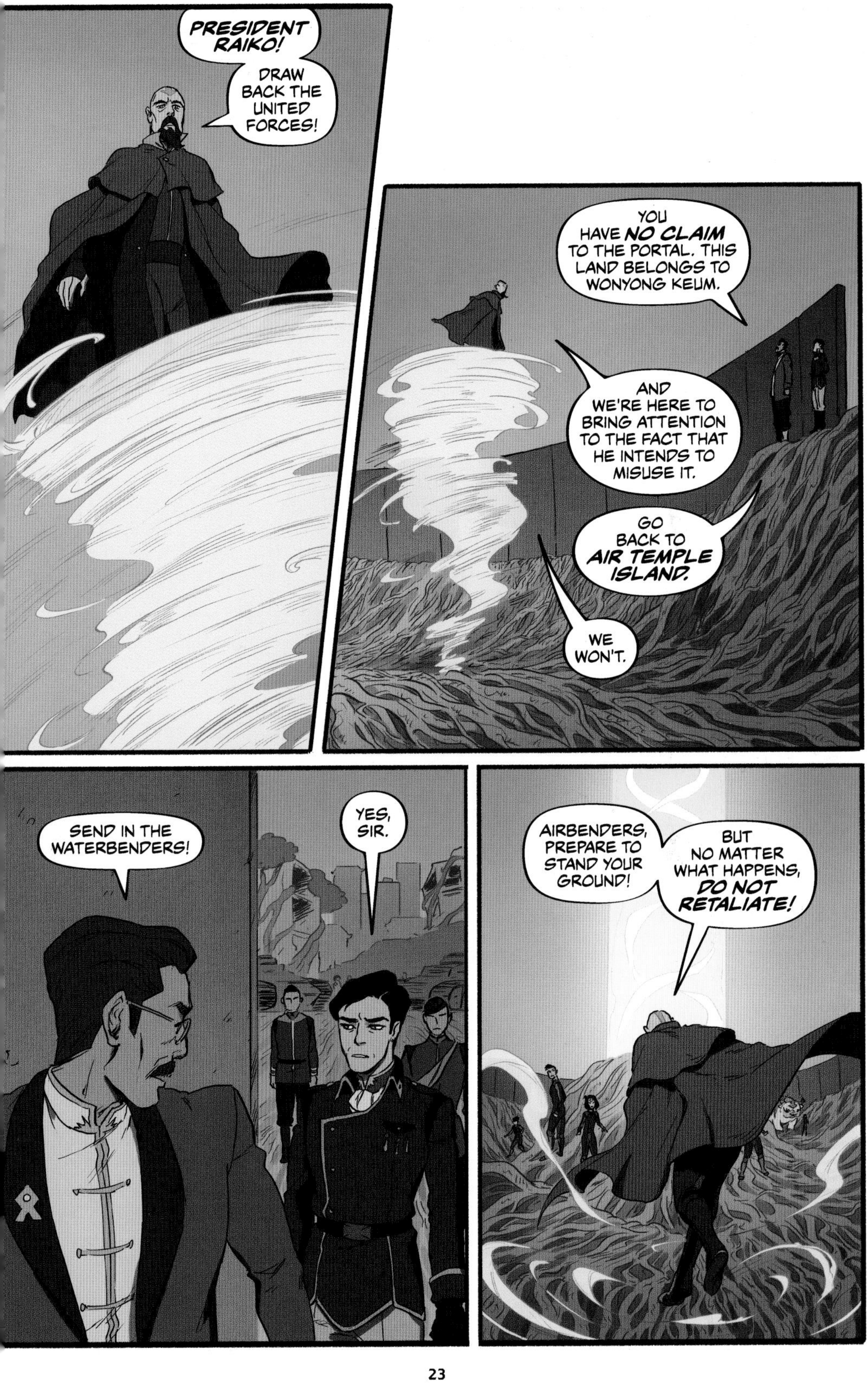
PRESIDENT RAIKO!
DRAW BACK THE UNITED FORCES!
YOU HAVE NO CLAIM TO THE PORTAL. THIS LAND BELONGS TO WONYONG KEUM.
AND WE'RE HERE TO BRING ATTENTION TO THE FACT THAT HE INTENDS TO MISUSE IT.
GO BACK TO AIR TEMPLE ISLAND.
WE WON'T.
SEND IN THE WATERBENDERS!
YES, SIR.
AIRBENDERS, PREPARE TO STAND YOUR GROUND!
BUT NO MATTER WHAT HAPPENS, DO NOT RETALIATE!

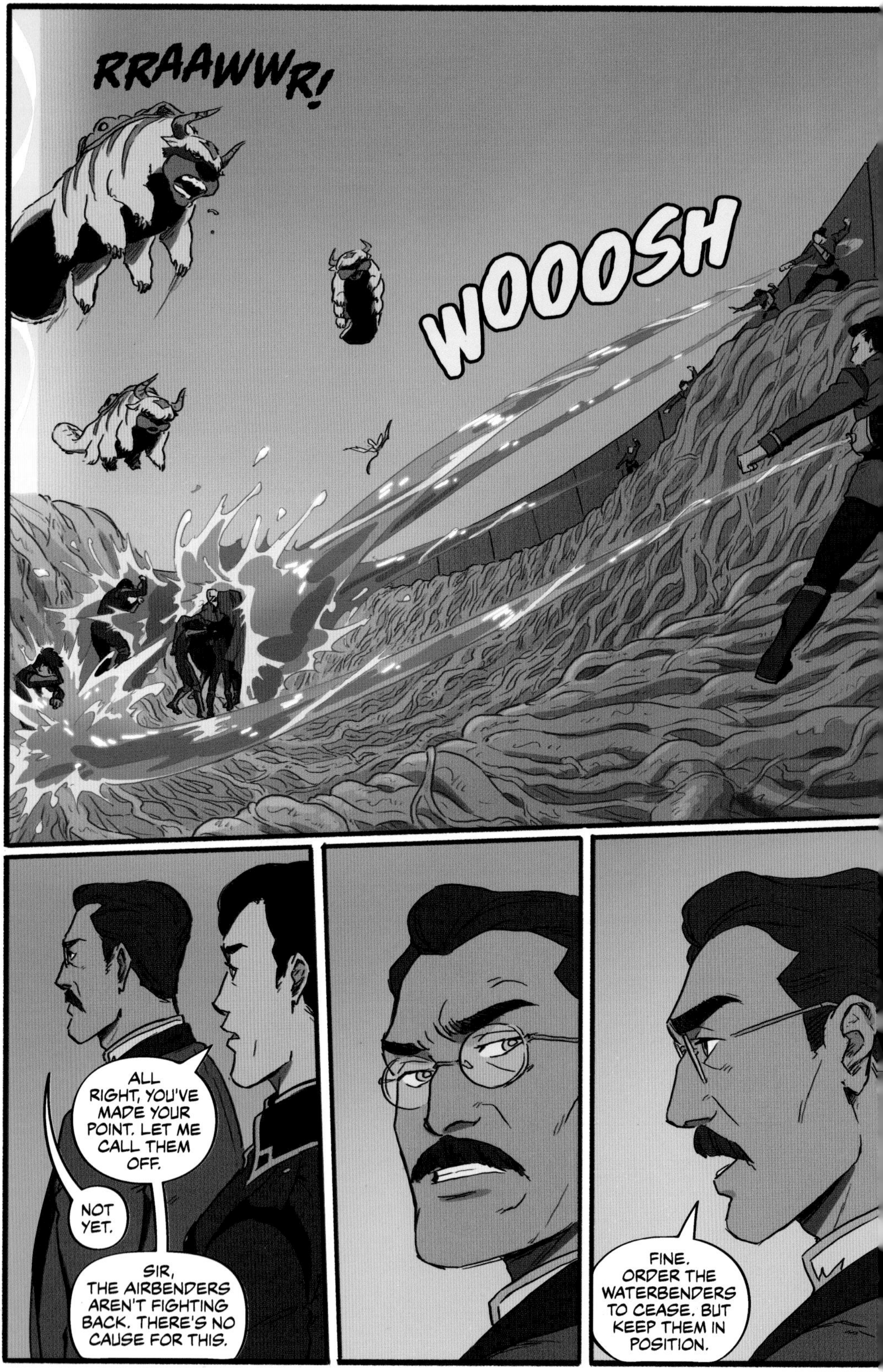
RRAAWWR!
WOOOSH
ALL RIGHT, YOU'VE MADE YOUR POINT. LET ME CALL THEM OFF.
NOT YET.
SIR, THE AIRBENDERS AREN'T FIGHTING BACK. THERE'S NO CAUSE FOR THIS.
FINE. ORDER THE WATERBENDERS TO CEASE. BUT KEEP THEM IN POSITION.

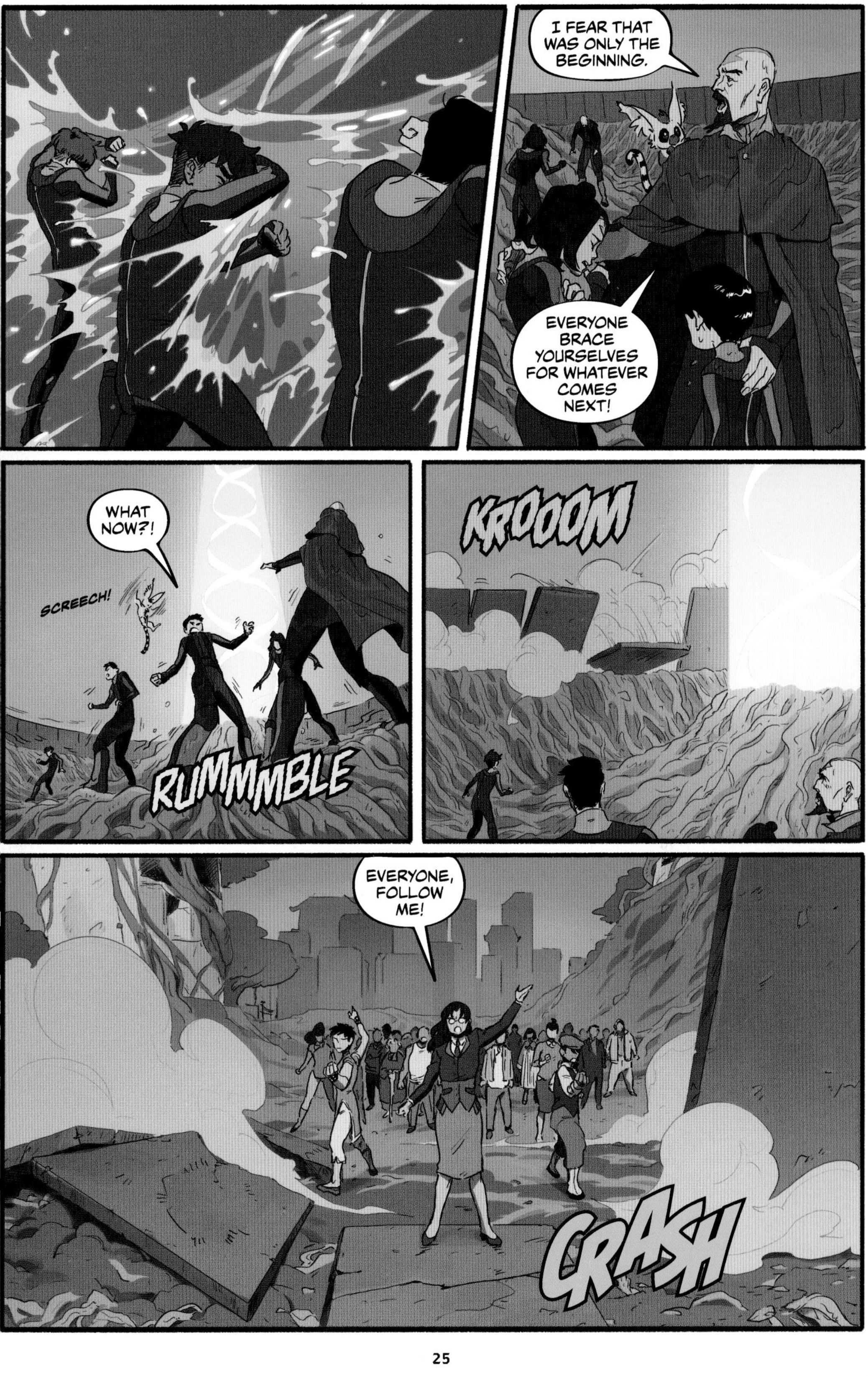
I FEAR THAT WAS ONLY THE BEGINNING.
EVERYONE BRACE YOURSELVES FOR WHATEVER COMES NEXT!
WHAT NOW?!
SCREECH!
RUMMMBLE
KROOOM
EVERYONE, FOLLOW ME!
CRASH

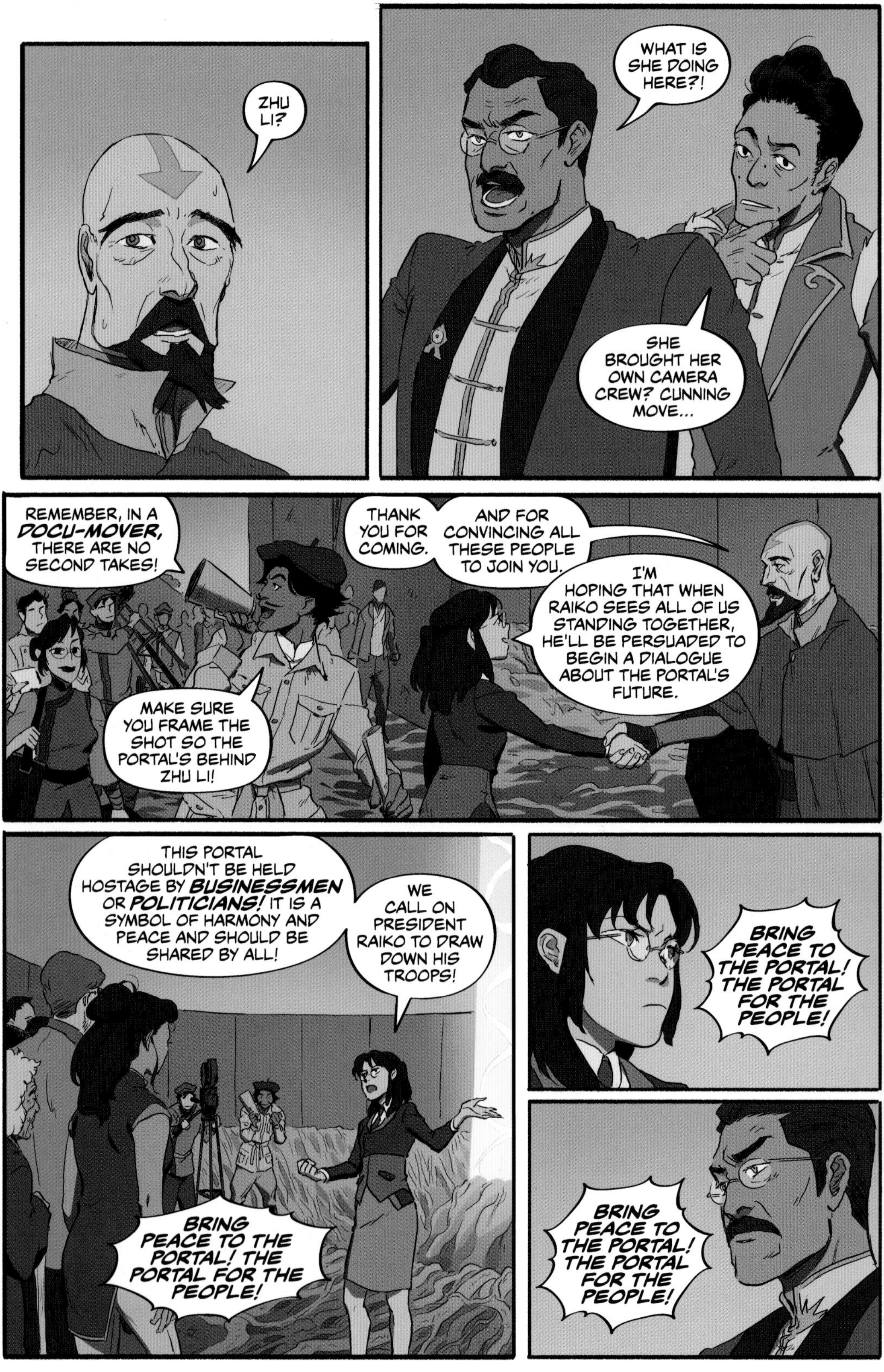
ZHU LI?
WHAT IS SHE DOING HERE?!
SHE BROUGHT HER OWN CAMERA CREW? CUNNING MOVE...
REMEMBER, IN A DOCU-MOVER, THERE ARE NO SECOND TAKES!
THANK YOU FOR COMING.
AND FOR CONVINCING ALL THESE PEOPLE TO JOIN YOU.
I'M HOPING THAT WHEN RAIKO SEES ALL OF US STANDING TOGETHER, HE'LL BE PERSUADED TO BEGIN A DIALOGUE ABOUT THE PORTAL'S FUTURE.
MAKE SURE YOU FRAME THE SHOT SO THE PORTAL'S BEHIND ZHU LI!
THIS PORTAL SHOULDN'T BE HELD HOSTAGE BY BUSINESSMEN OR POLITICIANS! IT IS A SYMBOL OF HARMONY AND PEACE AND SHOULD BE SHARED BY ALL!
WE CALL ON PRESIDENT RAIKO TO DRAW DOWN HIS TROOPS!
BRING PEACE TO THE PORTAL! THE PORTAL FOR THE PEOPLE!
BRING PEACE TO THE PORTAL! THE PORTAL FOR THE PEOPLE!
BRING PEACE TO THE PORTAL! THE PORTAL FOR THE PEOPLE!

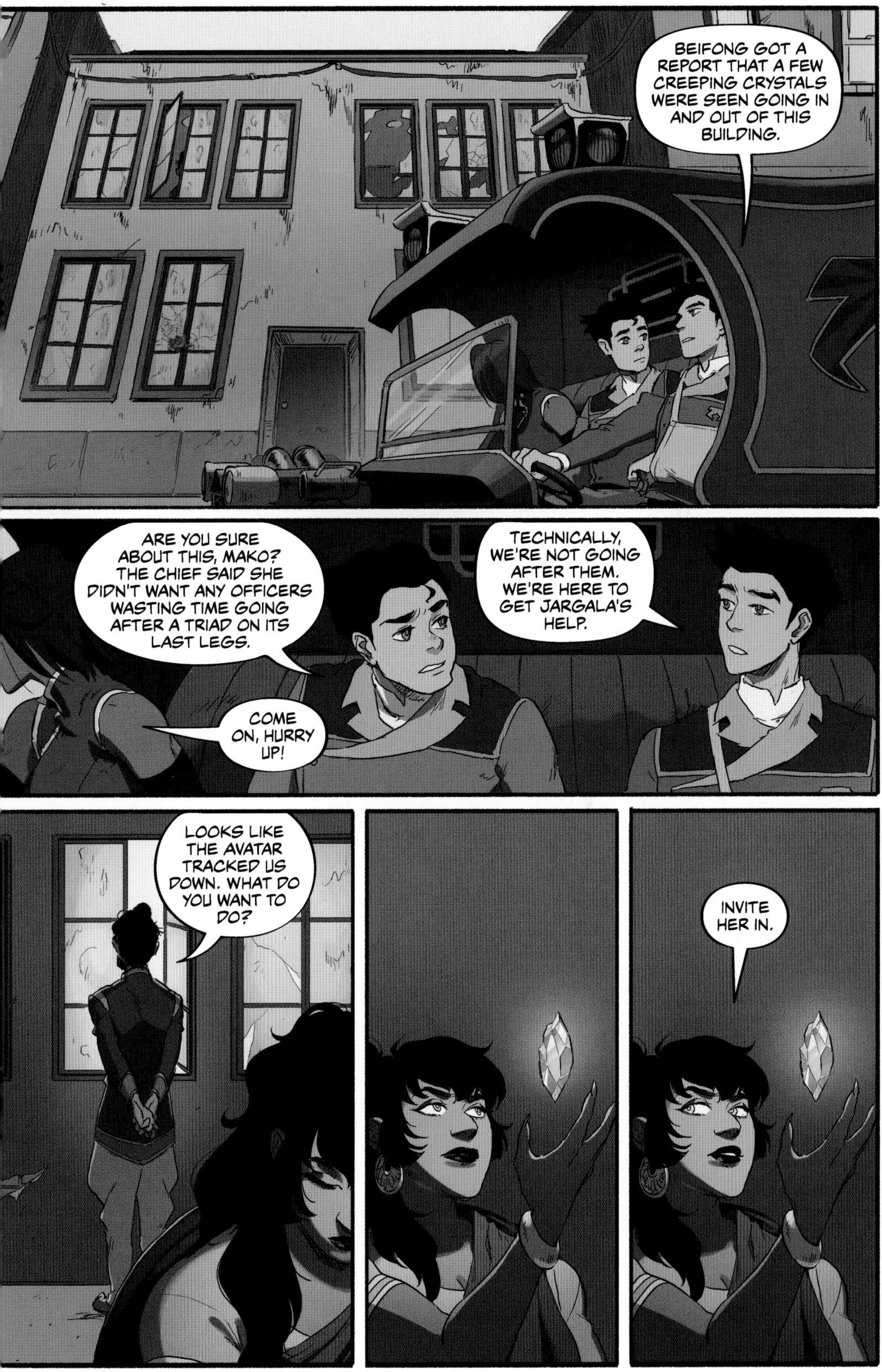
BEIFONG GOT A REPORT THAT A FEW CREEPING CRYSTALS WERE SEEN GOING IN AND OUT OF THIS BUILDING.
ARE YOU SURE ABOUT THIS, MAKO? THE CHIEF SAID SHE DIDN'T WANT ANY OFFICERS WASTING TIME GOING AFTER A TRIAD ON ITS LAST LEGS.
TECHNICALLY, WE'RE NOT GOING AFTER THEM. WE'RE HERE TO GET JARGALA'S HELP.
COME ON, HURRY UP!
LOOKS LIKE THE AVATAR TRACKED US DOWN. WHAT DO YOU WANT TO DO?
INVITE HER IN.

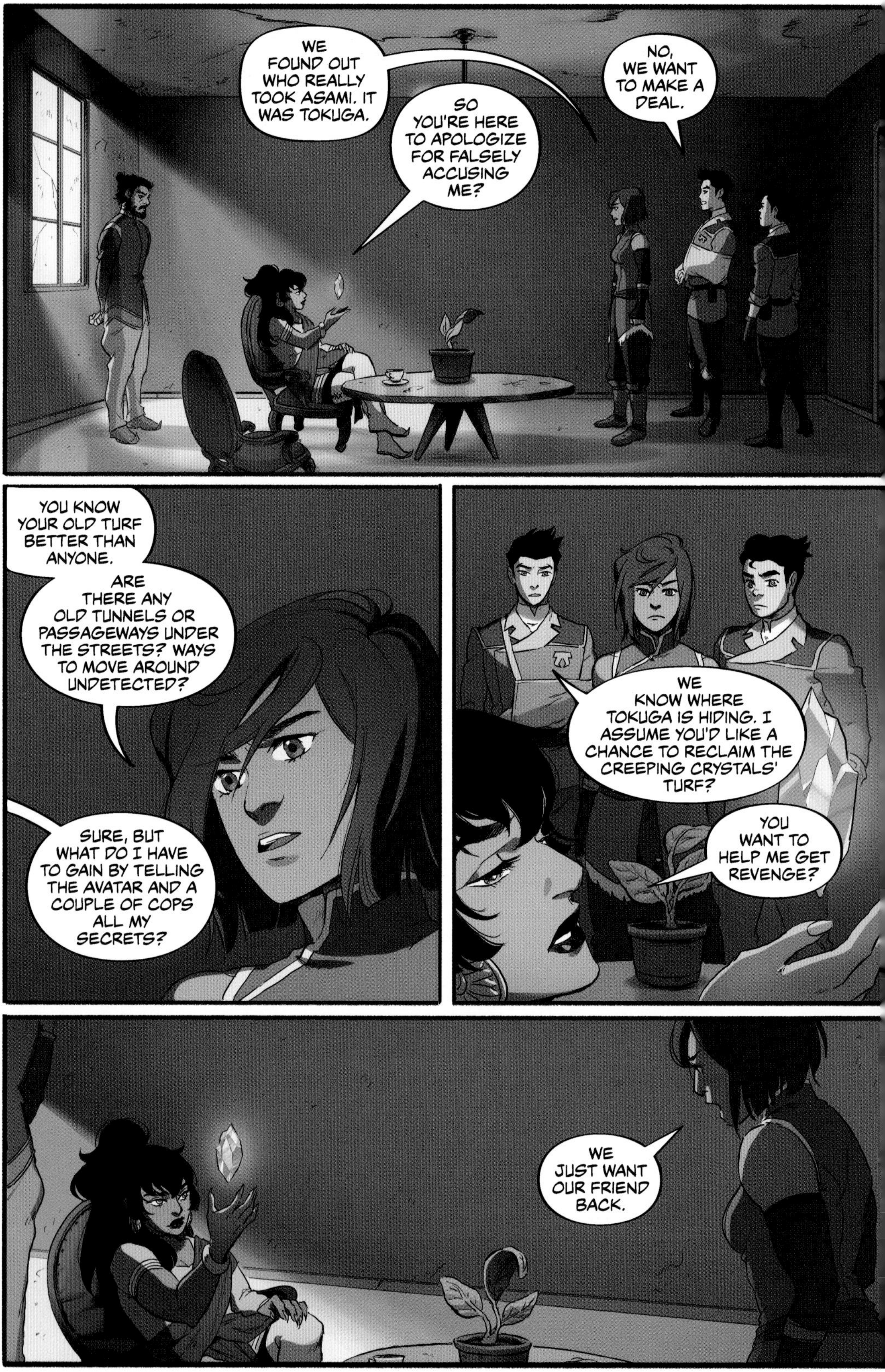
WE FOUND OUT WHO REALLY TOOK ASAMI. IT WAS TOKUGA.
SO YOU'RE HERE TO APOLOGIZE FOR FALSELY ACCUSING ME?
NO, WE WANT TO MAKE A DEAL.
YOU KNOW YOUR OLD TURF BETTER THAN ANYONE.
ARE THERE ANY OLD TUNNELS OR PASSAGEWAYS UNDER THE STREETS? WAYS TO MOVE AROUND UNDETECTED?
SURE, BUT WHAT DO I HAVE TO GAIN BY TELLING THE AVATAR AND A COUPLE OF COPS ALL MY SECRETS?
WE KNOW WHERE TOKUGA IS HIDING. I ASSUME YOU'D LIKE A CHANCE TO RECLAIM THE CREEPING CRYSTALS' TURF?
YOU WANT TO HELP ME GET REVENGE?
WE JUST WANT OUR FRIEND BACK.

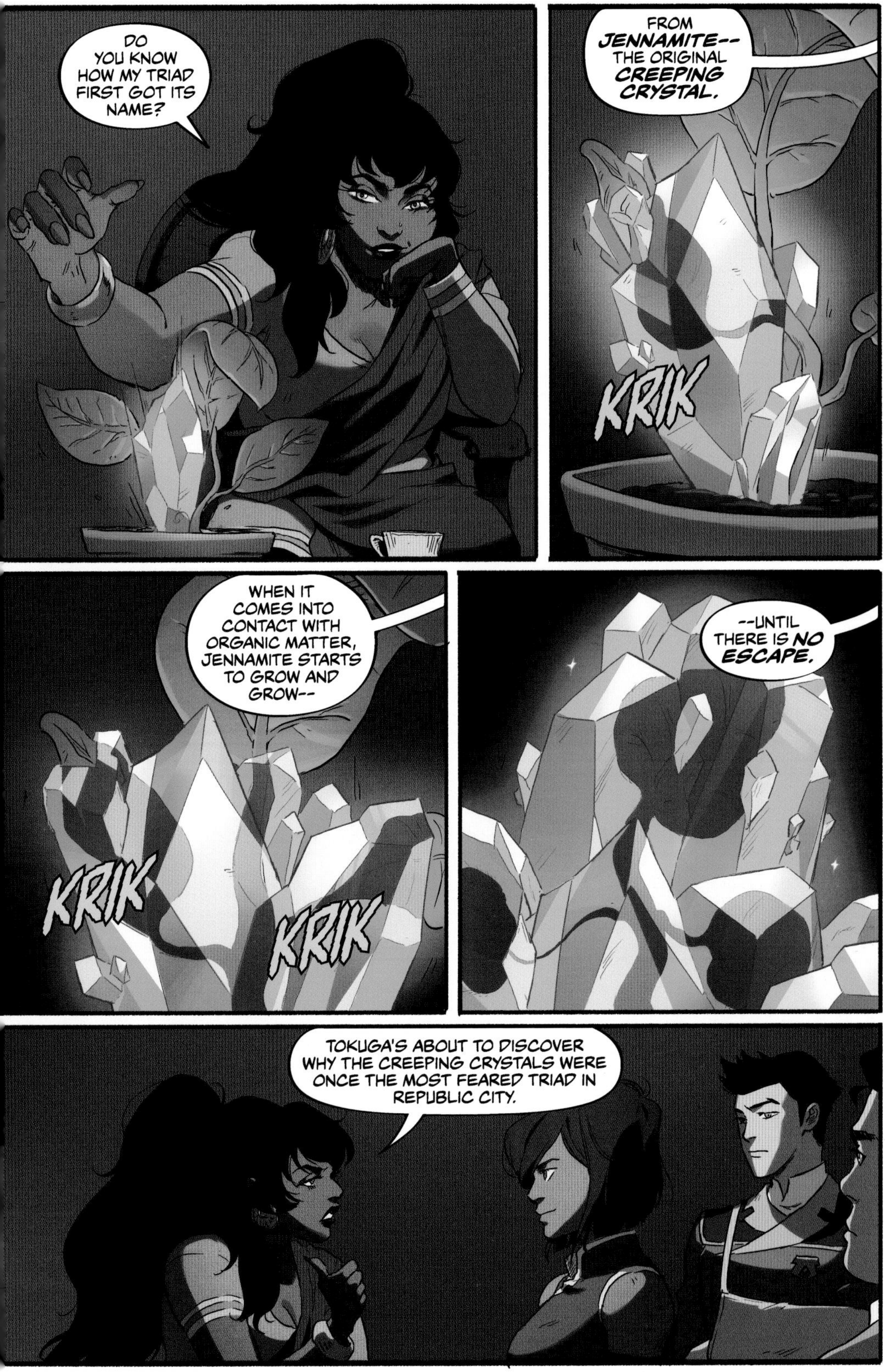
DO YOU KNOW HOW MY TRIAD FIRST GOT ITS NAME?
FROM JENNAMITE-- THE ORIGINAL CREEPING CRYSTAL.
KRIK
WHEN IT COMES INTO CONTACT WITH ORGANIC MATTER, JENNAMITE STARTS TO GROW AND GROW--
KRIK
KRIK
--UNTIL THERE IS NO ESCAPE.
TOKUGA'S ABOUT TO DISCOVER WHY THE CREEPING CRYSTALS WERE ONCE THE MOST FEARED TRIAD IN REPUBLIC CITY.

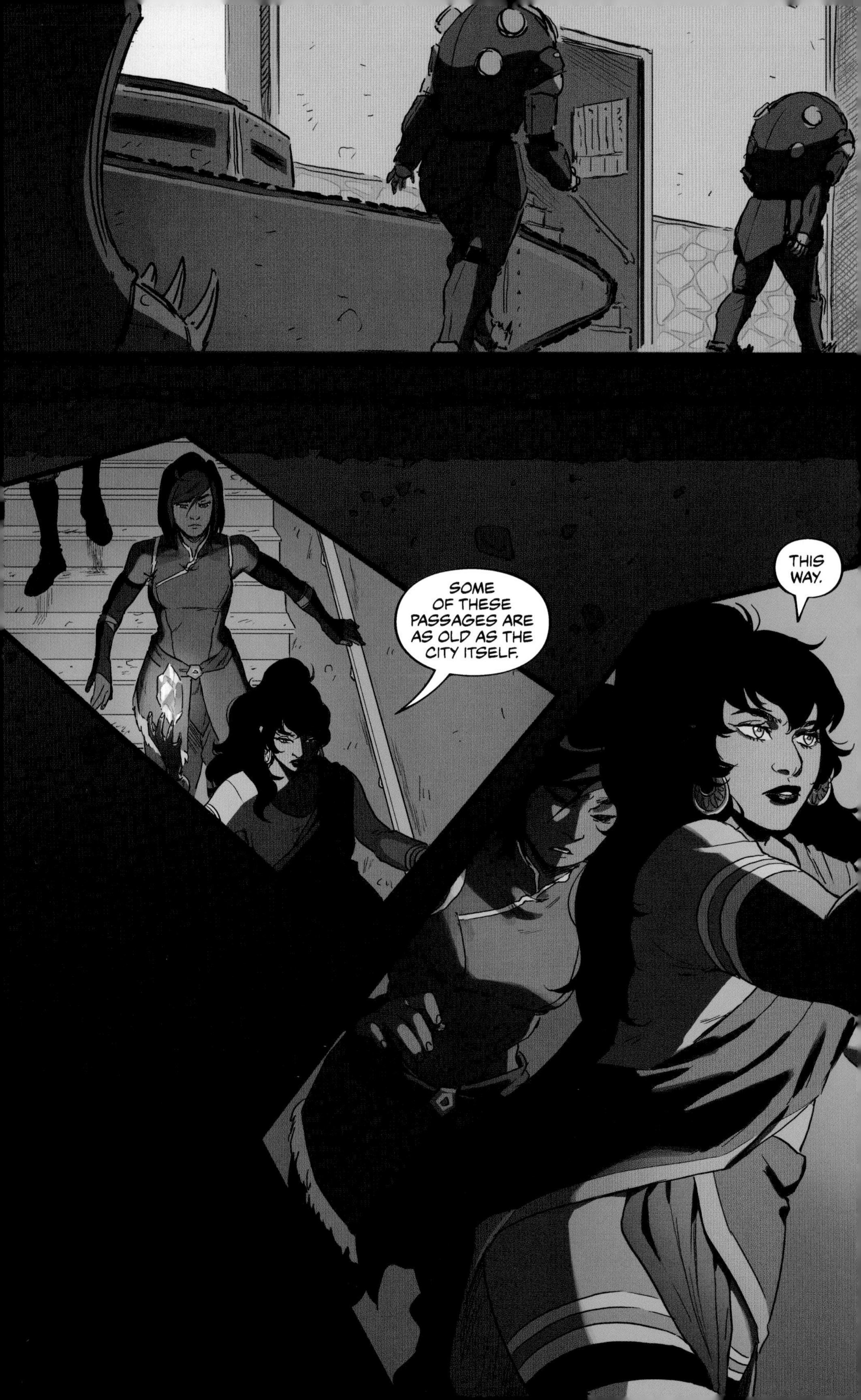
SOME OF THESE PASSAGES ARE AS OLD AS THE CITY ITSELF.
THIS WAY.

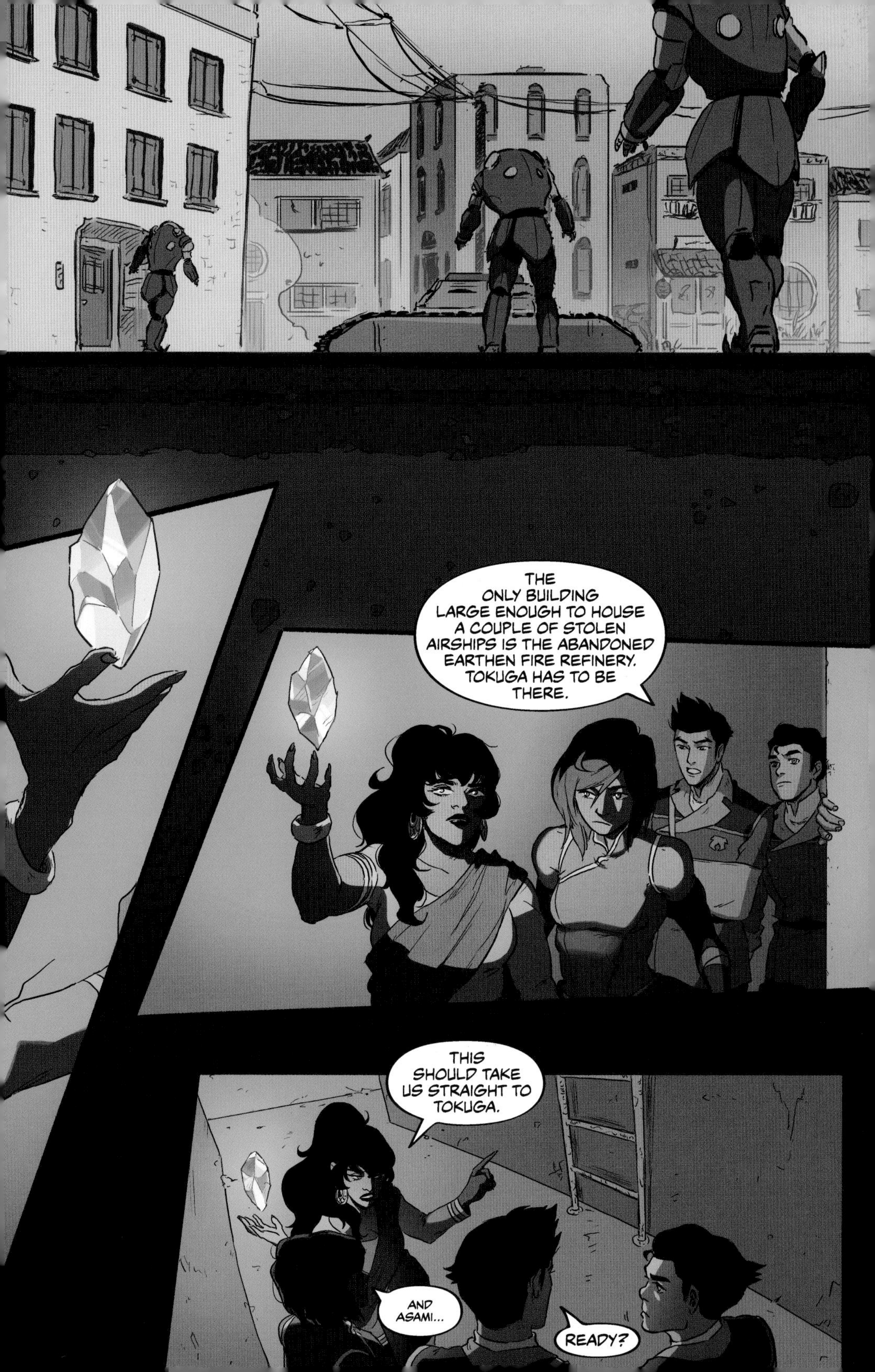
THE ONLY BUILDING LARGE ENOUGH TO HOUSE A COUPLE OF STOLEN AIRSHIPS IS THE ABANDONED EARTHEN FIRE REFINERY. TOKUGA HAS TO BE THERE.
THIS SHOULD TAKE US STRAIGHT TO TOKUGA.
AND ASAMI...
READY?

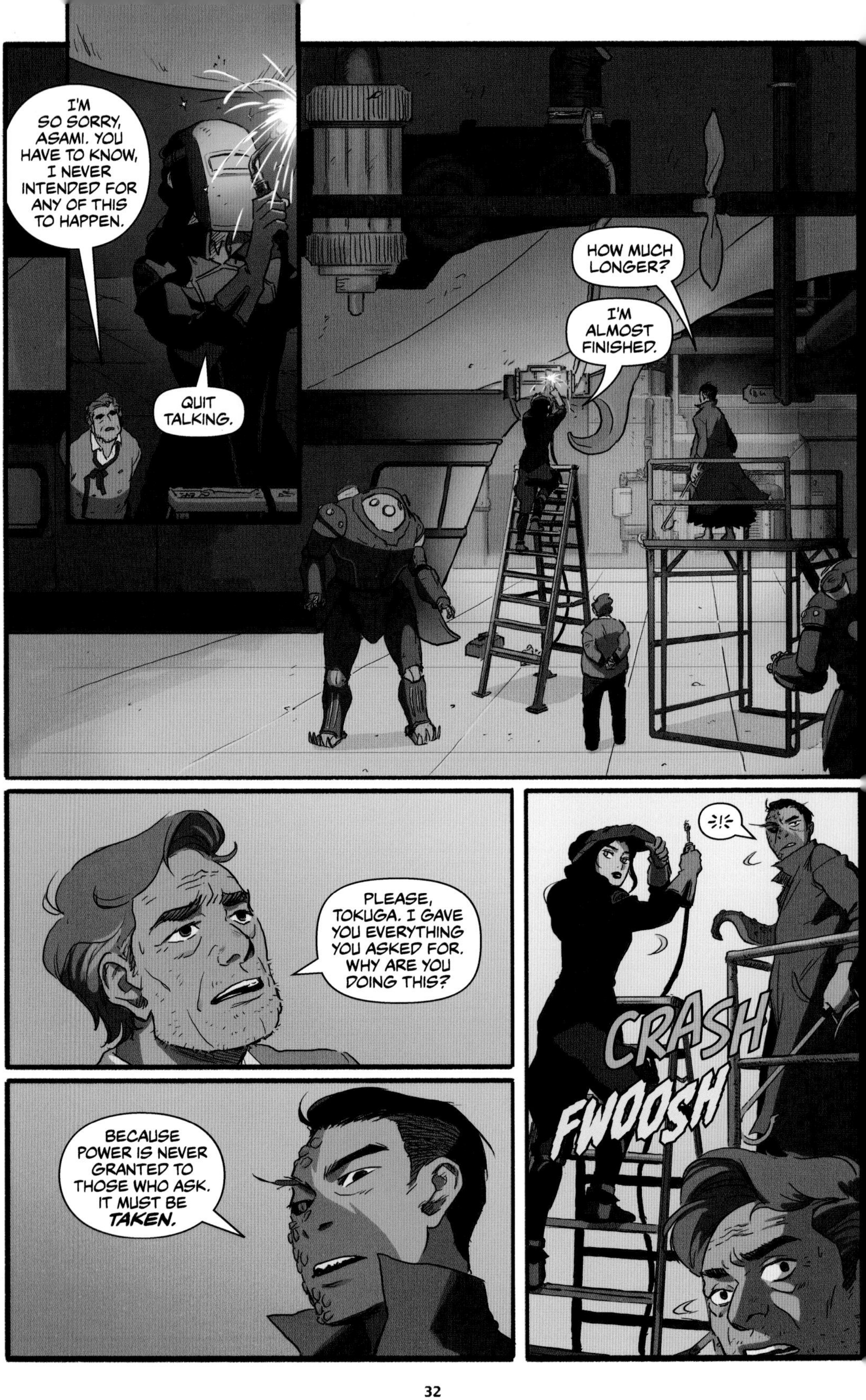

I'M SO SORRY, ASAMI. YOU HAVE TO KNOW, I NEVER INTENDED FOR ANY OF THIS TO HAPPEN.
QUIT TALKING.
HOW MUCH LONGER?
I'M ALMOST FINISHED.
PLEASE, TOKUGA. I GAVE YOU EVERYTHING YOU ASKED FOR. WHY ARE YOU DOING THIS?
BECAUSE POWER IS NEVER GRANTED TO THOSE WHO ASK. IT MUST BE *TAKEN.*
!
CRASH
FWOOSH

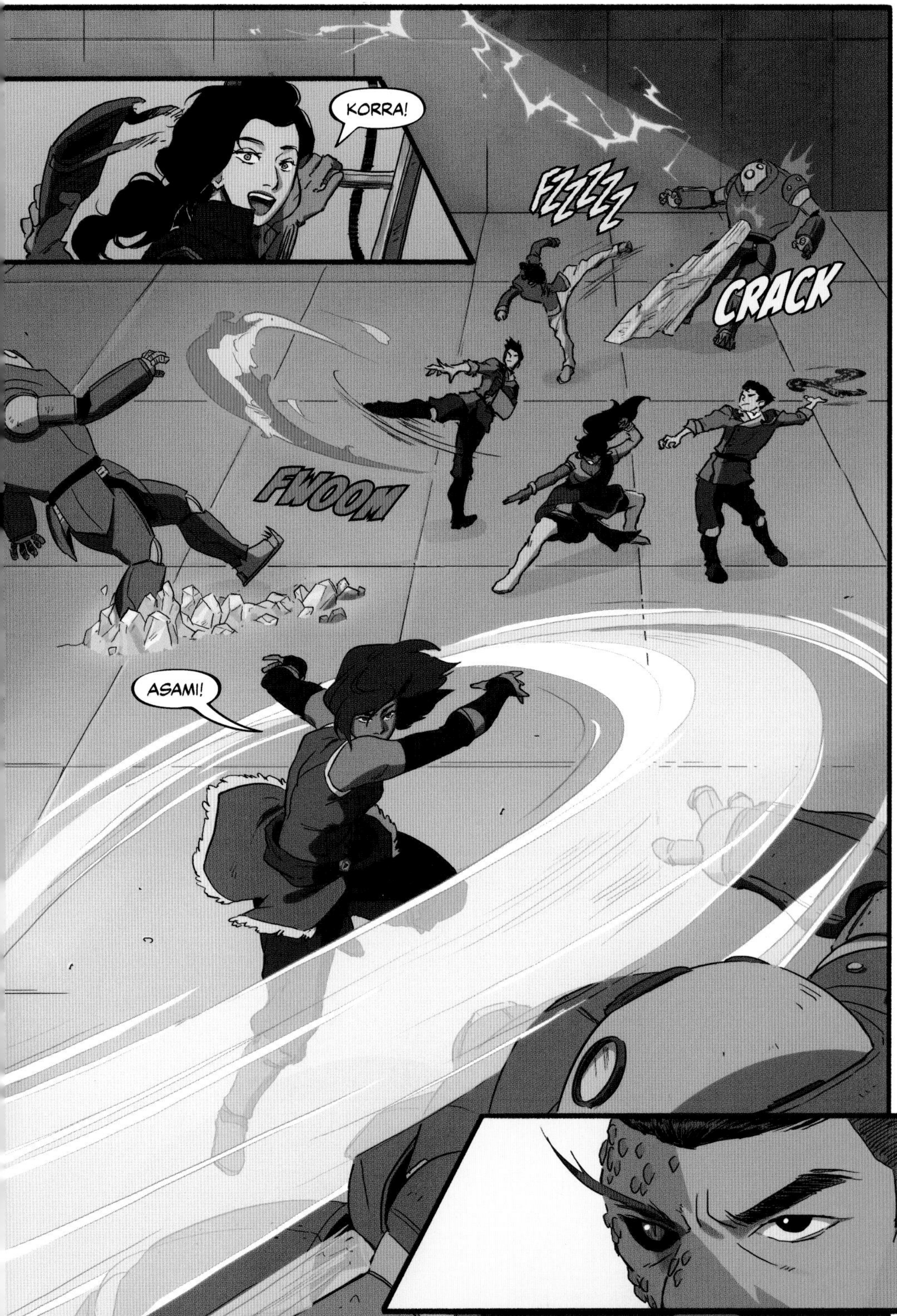
KORRA!
FZZZZZ
CRACK
FWOOM
ASAMI!

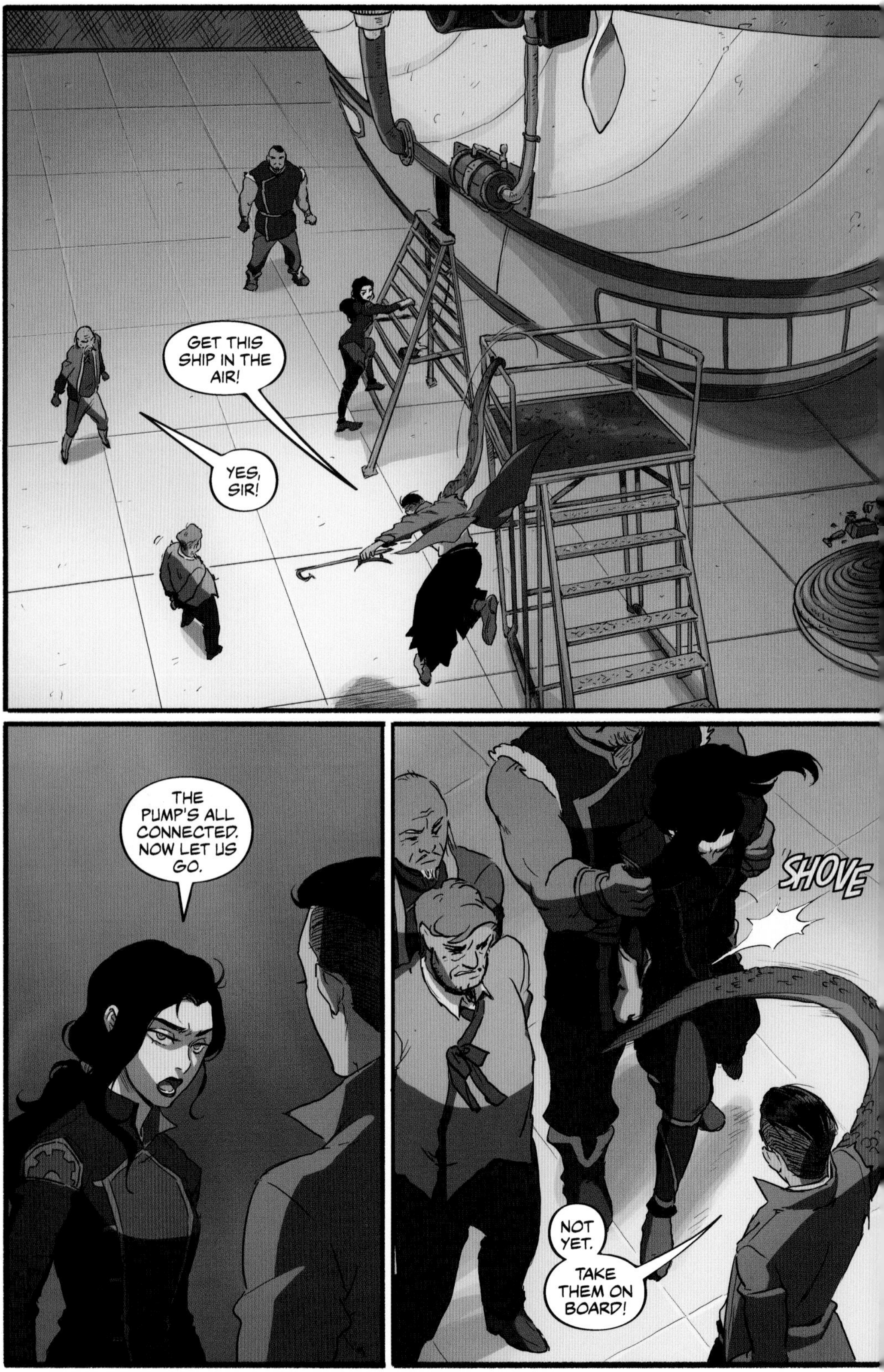
GET THIS SHIP IN THE AIR!
YES, SIR!
THE PUMP'S ALL CONNECTED. NOW LET US GO.
SHOVE
NOT YET.
TAKE THEM ON BOARD!

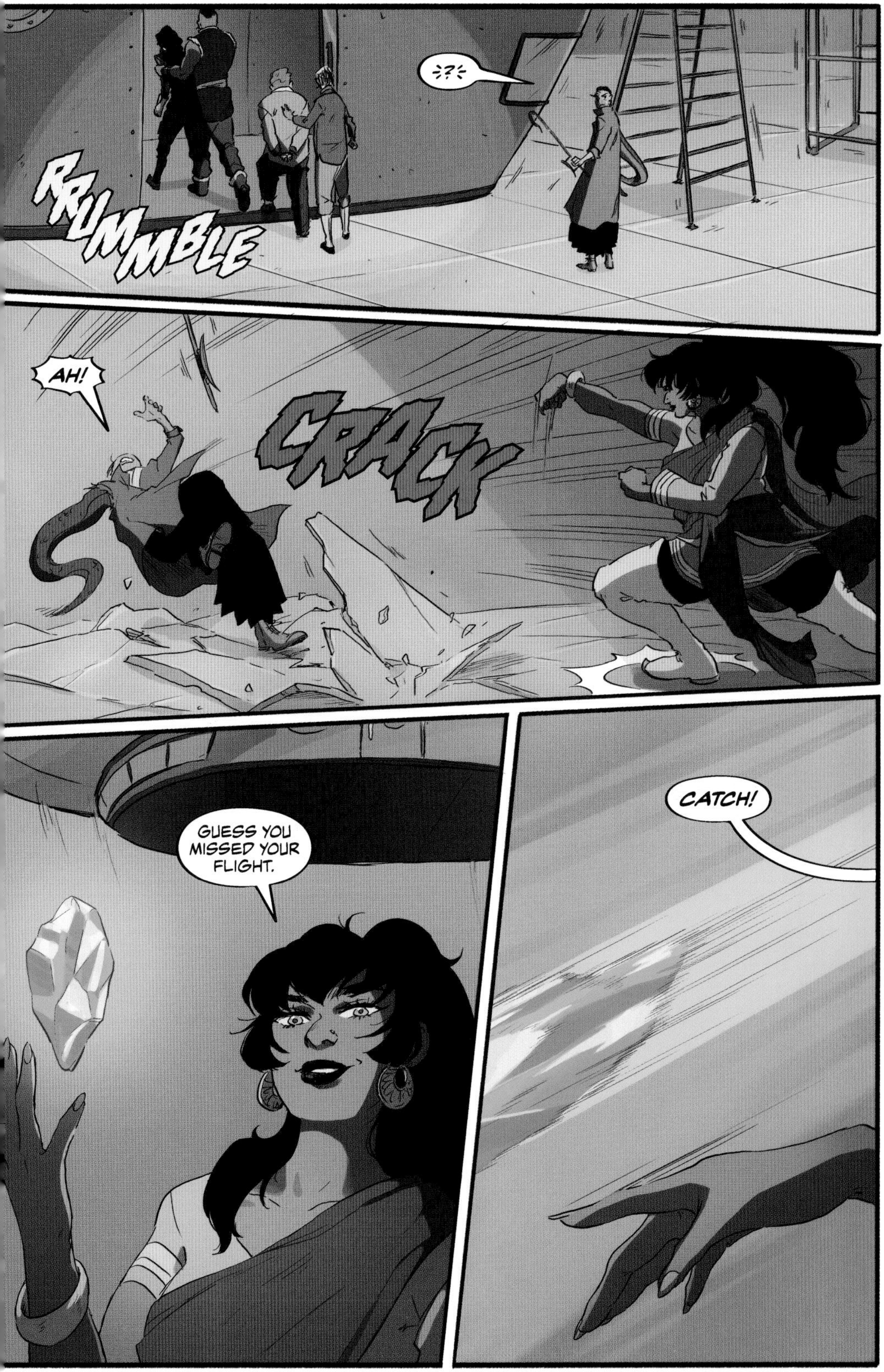
!?!
RRUMMBLE
AH!
CRACK
GUESS YOU MISSED YOUR FLIGHT.
CATCH!

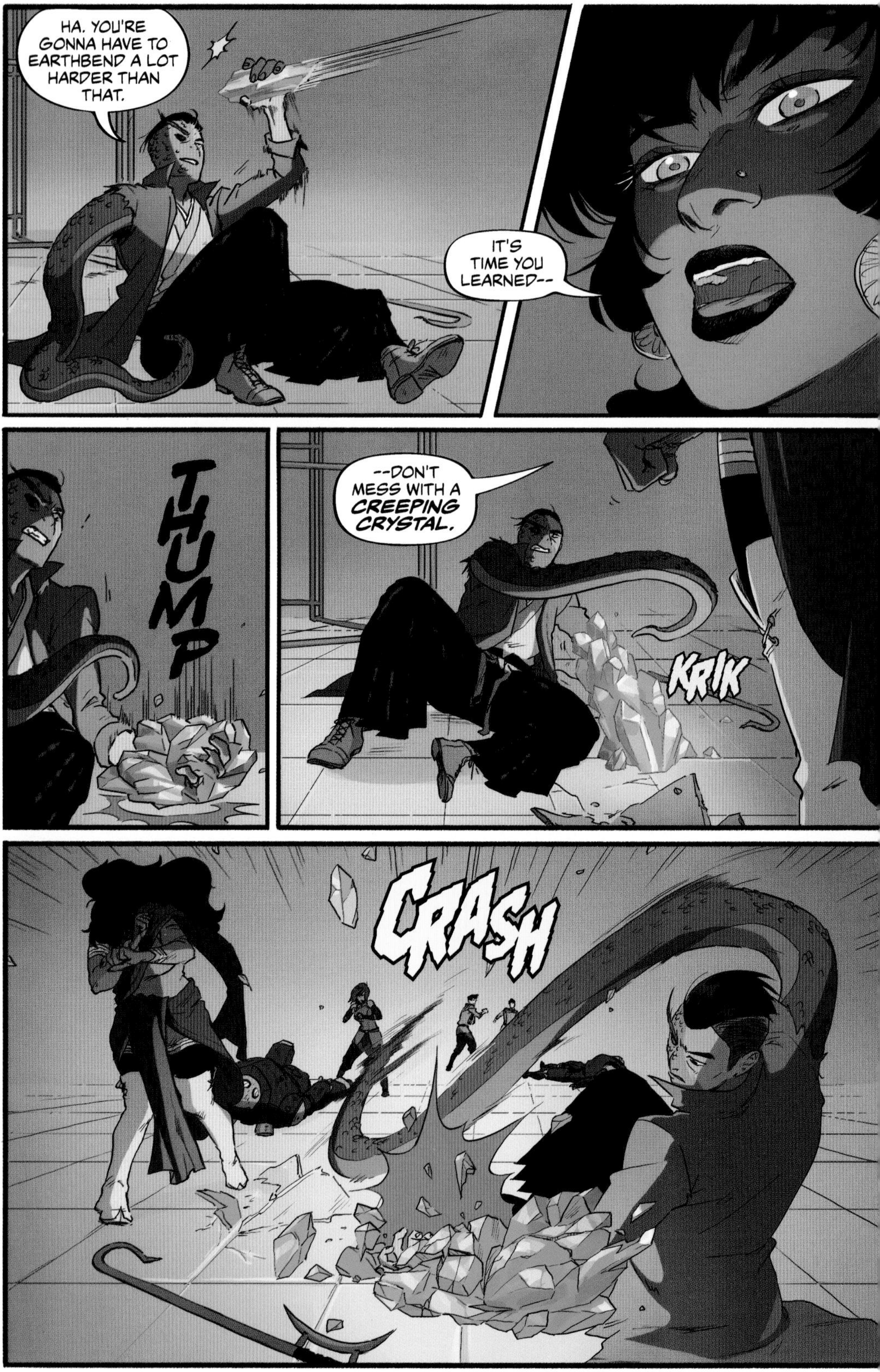
HA. YOU'RE GONNA HAVE TO EARTHBEND A LOT HARDER THAN THAT.
IT'S TIME YOU LEARNED--
THUMP
--DON'T MESS WITH A CREEPING CRYSTAL.
KRIK
CRASH

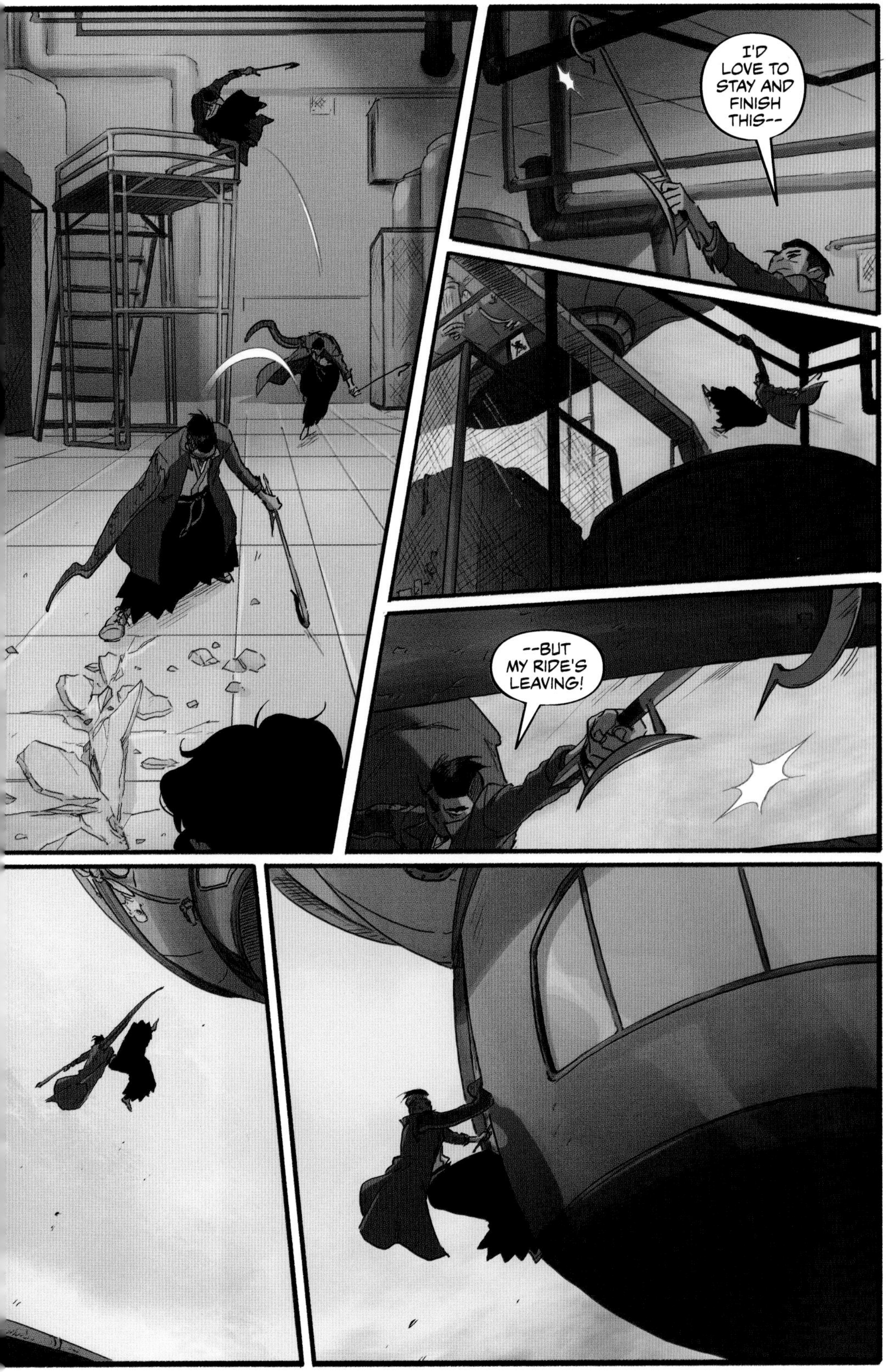
I'D LOVE TO STAY AND FINISH THIS--
--BUT MY RIDE'S LEAVING!

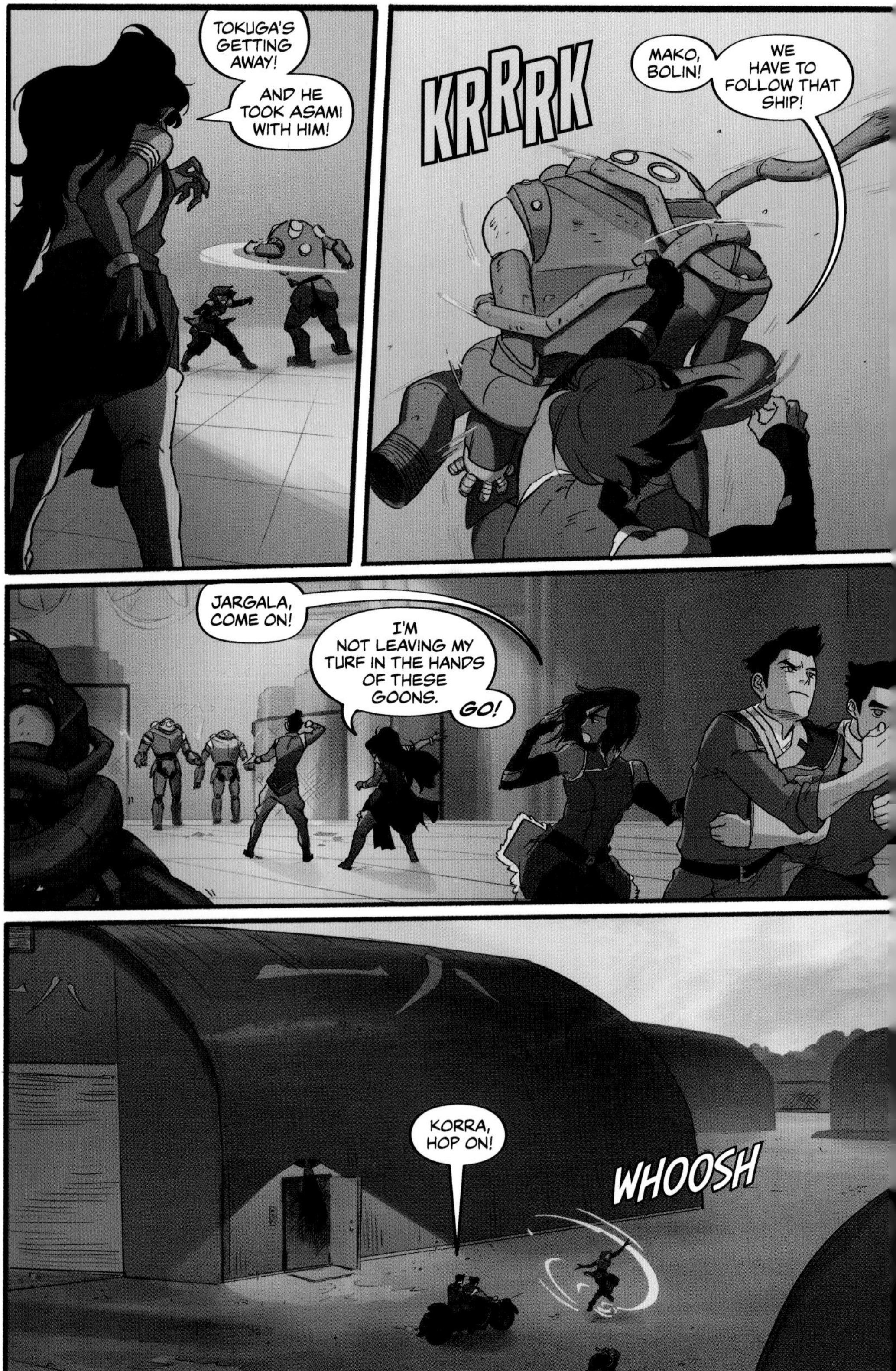
TOKUGA'S GETTING AWAY!
AND HE TOOK ASAMI WITH HIM!
KRRRK
MAKO, BOLIN!
WE HAVE TO FOLLOW THAT SHIP!
JARGALA, COME ON!
I'M NOT LEAVING MY TURF IN THE HANDS OF THESE GOONS.
GO!
KORRA, HOP ON!
WHOOSH

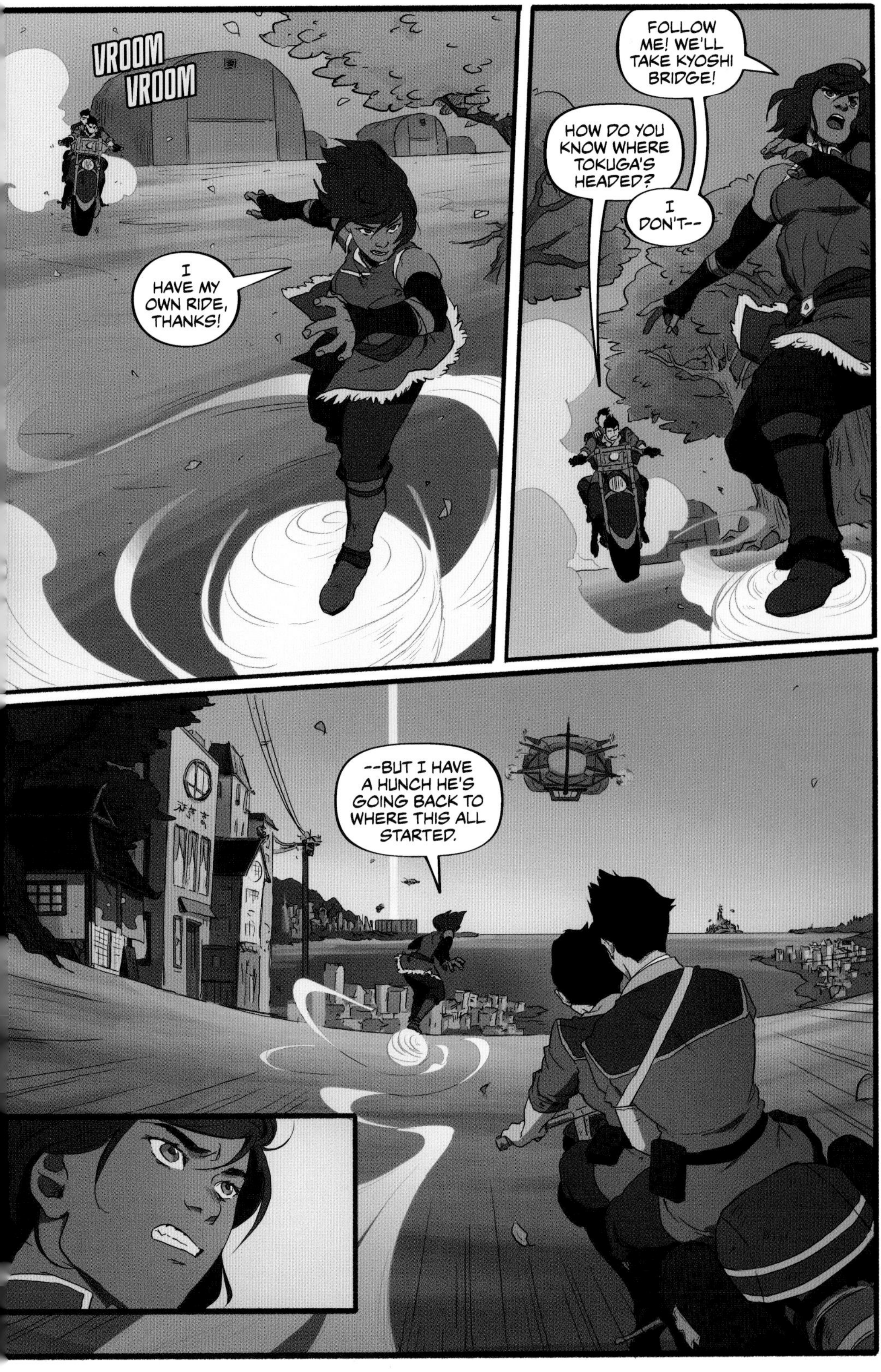
VROOM
VROOM
I HAVE MY OWN RIDE, THANKS!
FOLLOW ME! WE'LL TAKE KYOSHI BRIDGE!
HOW DO YOU KNOW WHERE TOKUGA'S HEADED?
I DON'T--
--BUT I HAVE A HUNCH HE'S GOING BACK TO WHERE THIS ALL STARTED.

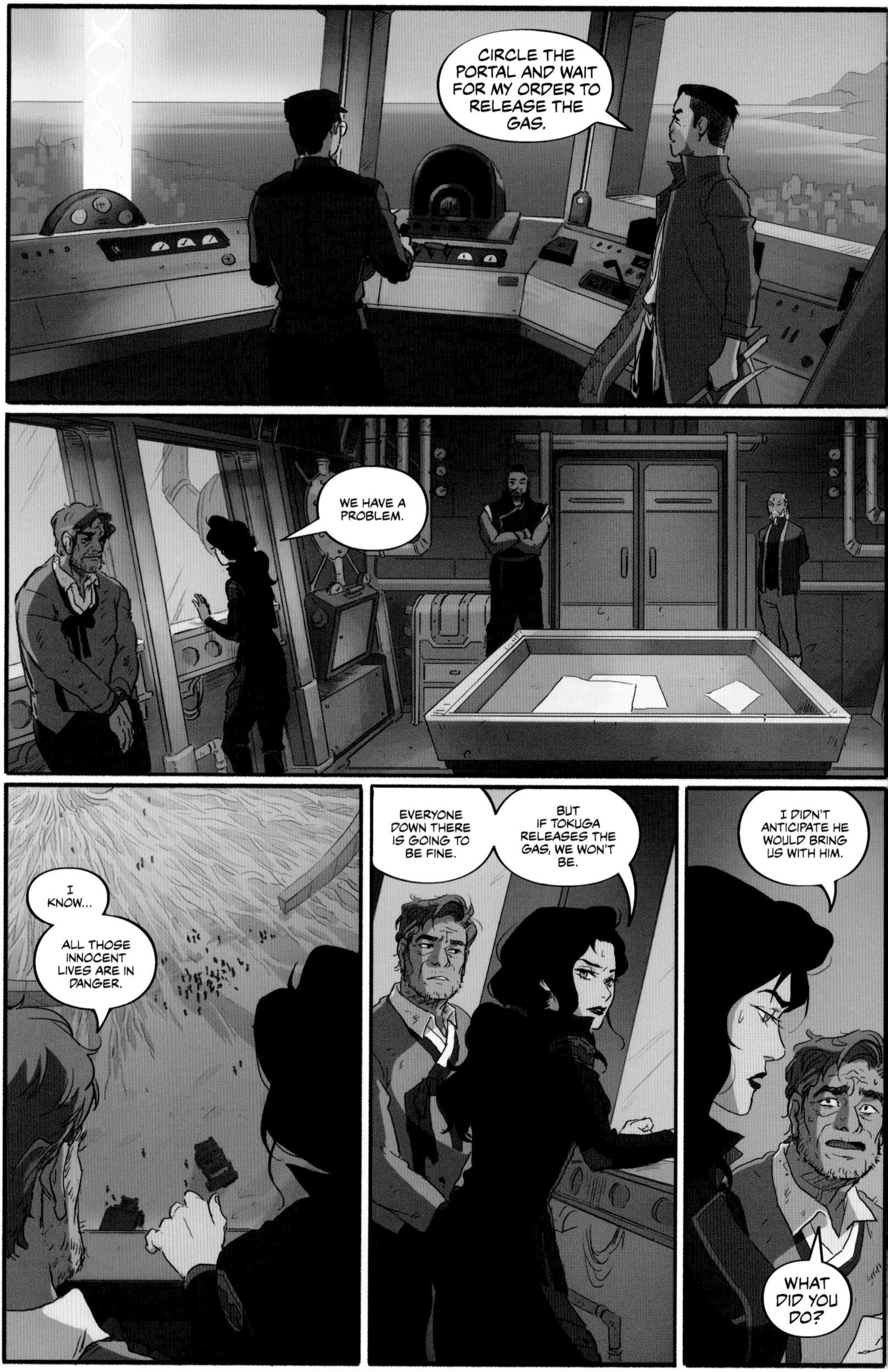
CIRCLE THE PORTAL AND WAIT FOR MY ORDER TO RELEASE THE GAS.
WE HAVE A PROBLEM.
I KNOW...
ALL THOSE INNOCENT LIVES ARE IN DANGER.
EVERYONE DOWN THERE IS GOING TO BE FINE.
BUT IF TOKUGA RELEASES THE GAS, WE WON'T BE.
I DIDN'T ANTICIPATE HE WOULD BRING US WITH HIM.
WHAT DID YOU DO?

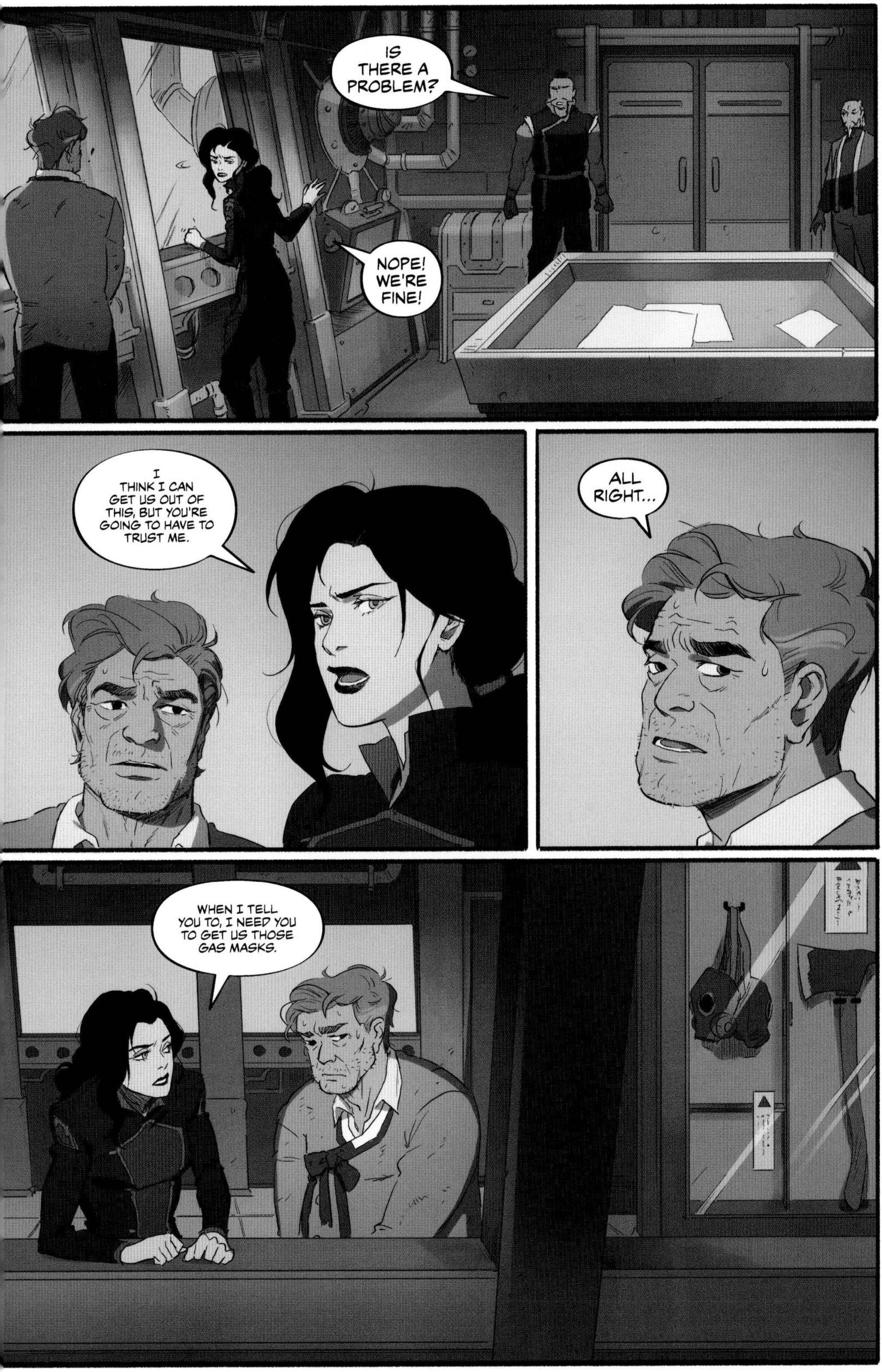
IS THERE A PROBLEM?
NOPE! WE'RE FINE!
I THINK I CAN GET US OUT OF THIS, BUT YOU'RE GOING TO HAVE TO TRUST ME.
ALL RIGHT...
WHEN I TELL YOU TO, I NEED YOU TO GET US THOSE GAS MASKS.

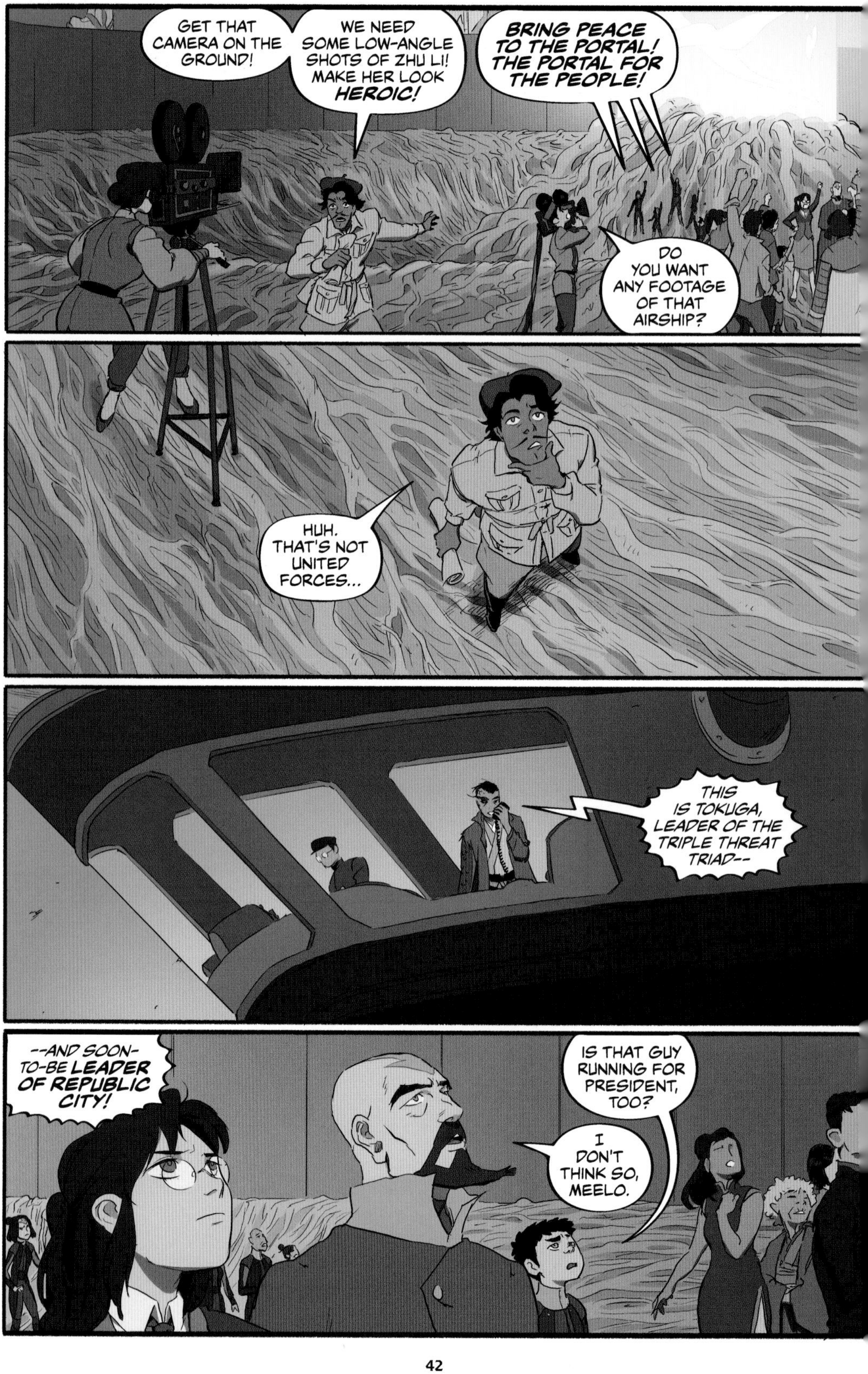
GET THAT CAMERA ON THE GROUND!
WE NEED SOME LOW-ANGLE SHOTS OF ZHU LI! MAKE HER LOOK HEROIC!
BRING PEACE TO THE PORTAL! THE PORTAL FOR THE PEOPLE!
DO YOU WANT ANY FOOTAGE OF THAT AIRSHIP?
HUH. THAT'S NOT UNITED FORCES...
THIS IS TOKUGA, LEADER OF THE TRIPLE THREAT TRIAD--
--AND SOON-TO-BE LEADER OF REPUBLIC CITY!
IS THAT GUY RUNNING FOR PRESIDENT, TOO?
I DON'T THINK SO, MEELO.

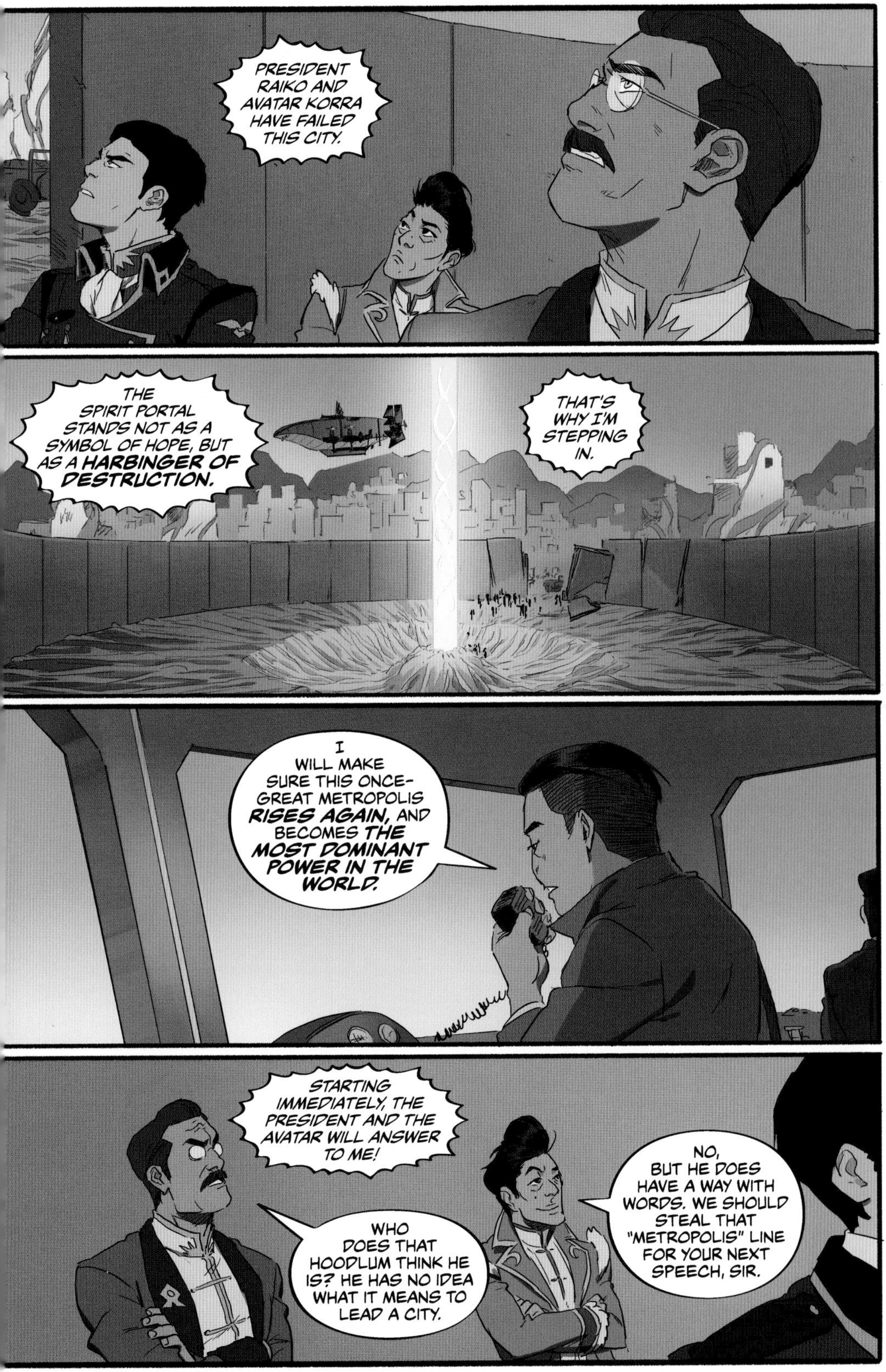
PRESIDENT RAIKO AND AVATAR KORRA HAVE FAILED THIS CITY.
THE SPIRIT PORTAL STANDS NOT AS A SYMBOL OF HOPE, BUT AS A HARBINGER OF DESTRUCTION.
THAT'S WHY I'M STEPPING IN.
I WILL MAKE SURE THIS ONCE-GREAT METROPOLIS RISES AGAIN, AND BECOMES THE MOST DOMINANT POWER IN THE WORLD.
STARTING IMMEDIATELY, THE PRESIDENT AND THE AVATAR WILL ANSWER TO ME!
WHO DOES THAT HOODLUM THINK HE IS? HE HAS NO IDEA WHAT IT MEANS TO LEAD A CITY.
NO, BUT HE DOES HAVE A WAY WITH WORDS. WE SHOULD STEAL THAT "METROPOLIS" LINE FOR YOUR NEXT SPEECH, SIR.

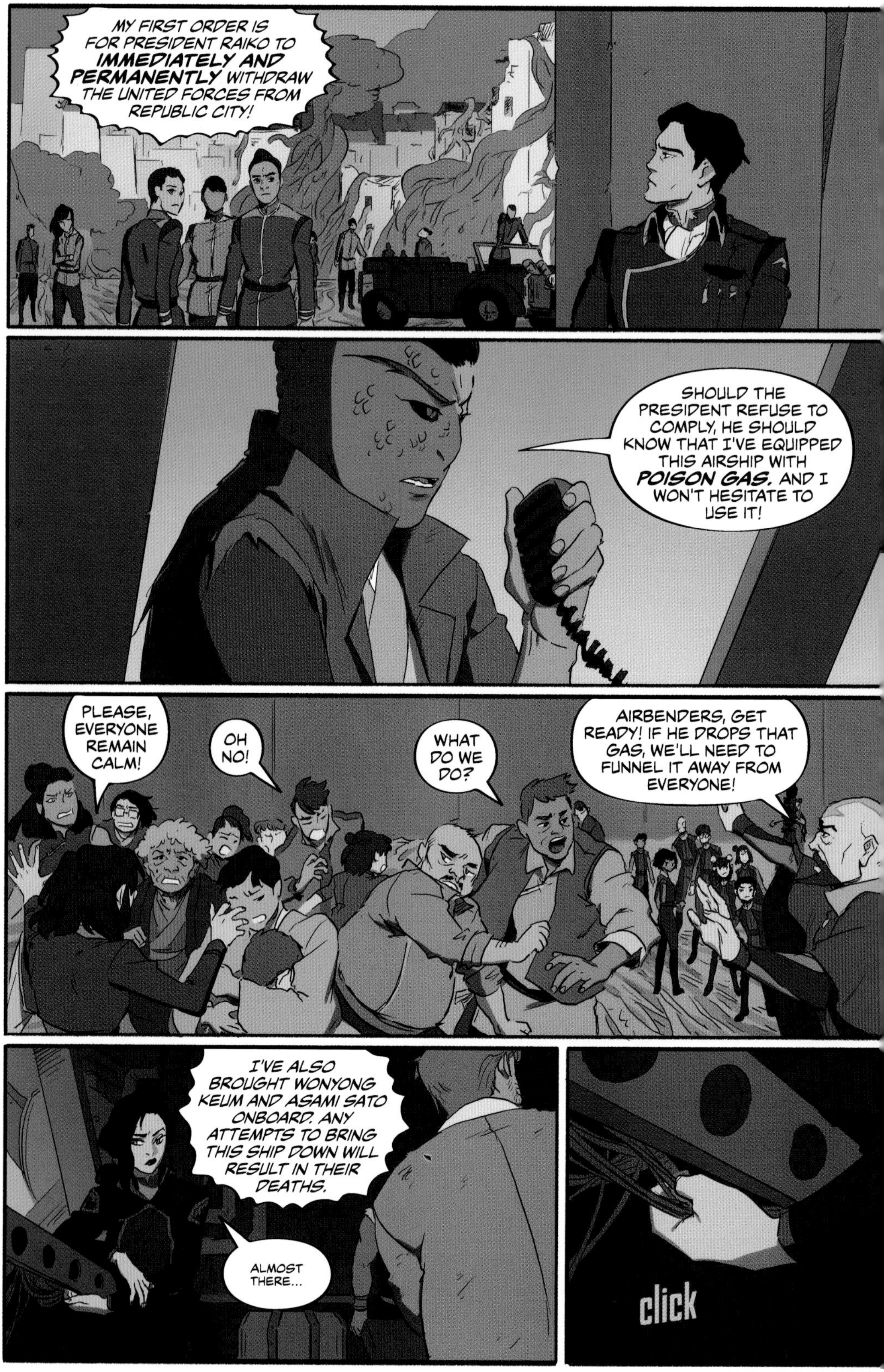
MY FIRST ORDER IS FOR PRESIDENT RAIKO TO IMMEDIATELY AND PERMANENTLY WITHDRAW THE UNITED FORCES FROM REPUBLIC CITY!
SHOULD THE PRESIDENT REFUSE TO COMPLY, HE SHOULD KNOW THAT I'VE EQUIPPED THIS AIRSHIP WITH POISON GAS. AND I WON'T HESITATE TO USE IT!
PLEASE, EVERYONE REMAIN CALM!
OH NO!
WHAT DO WE DO?
AIRBENDERS, GET READY! IF HE DROPS THAT GAS, WE'LL NEED TO FUNNEL IT AWAY FROM EVERYONE!
I'VE ALSO BROUGHT WONYONG KEUM AND ASAMI SATO ONBOARD. ANY ATTEMPTS TO BRING THIS SHIP DOWN WILL RESULT IN THEIR DEATHS.
ALMOST THERE...
click

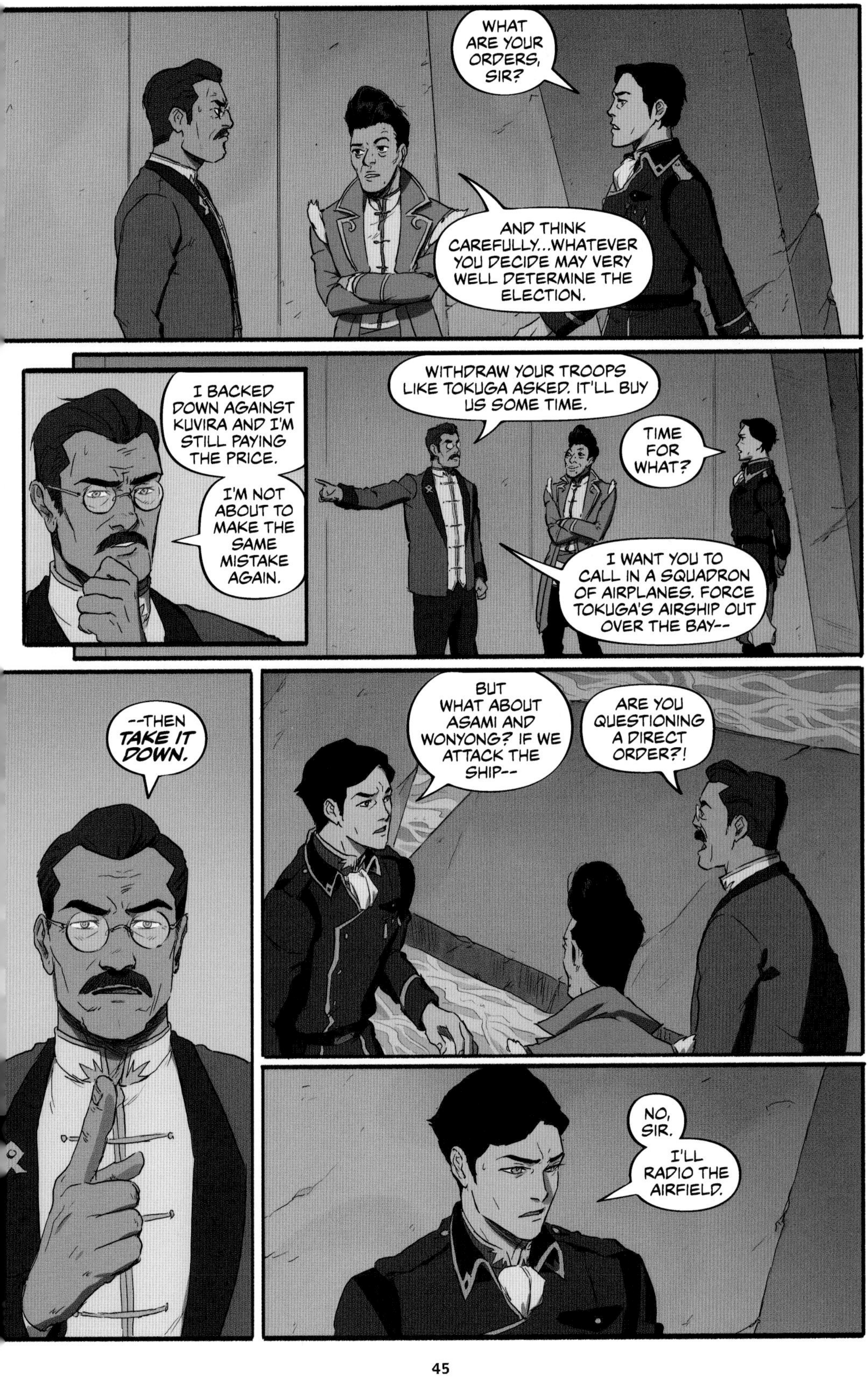
WHAT ARE YOUR ORDERS, SIR?
AND THINK CAREFULLY...WHATEVER YOU DECIDE MAY VERY WELL DETERMINE THE ELECTION.
I BACKED DOWN AGAINST KUVIRA AND I'M STILL PAYING THE PRICE.
I'M NOT ABOUT TO MAKE THE SAME MISTAKE AGAIN.
WITHDRAW YOUR TROOPS LIKE TOKUGA ASKED. IT'LL BUY US SOME TIME.
TIME FOR WHAT?
I WANT YOU TO CALL IN A SQUADRON OF AIRPLANES. FORCE TOKUGA'S AIRSHIP OUT OVER THE BAY--
--THEN *TAKE IT DOWN.*
BUT WHAT ABOUT ASAMI AND WONYONG? IF WE ATTACK THE SHIP--
ARE YOU QUESTIONING A DIRECT ORDER?!
NO, SIR.
I'LL RADIO THE AIRFIELD.

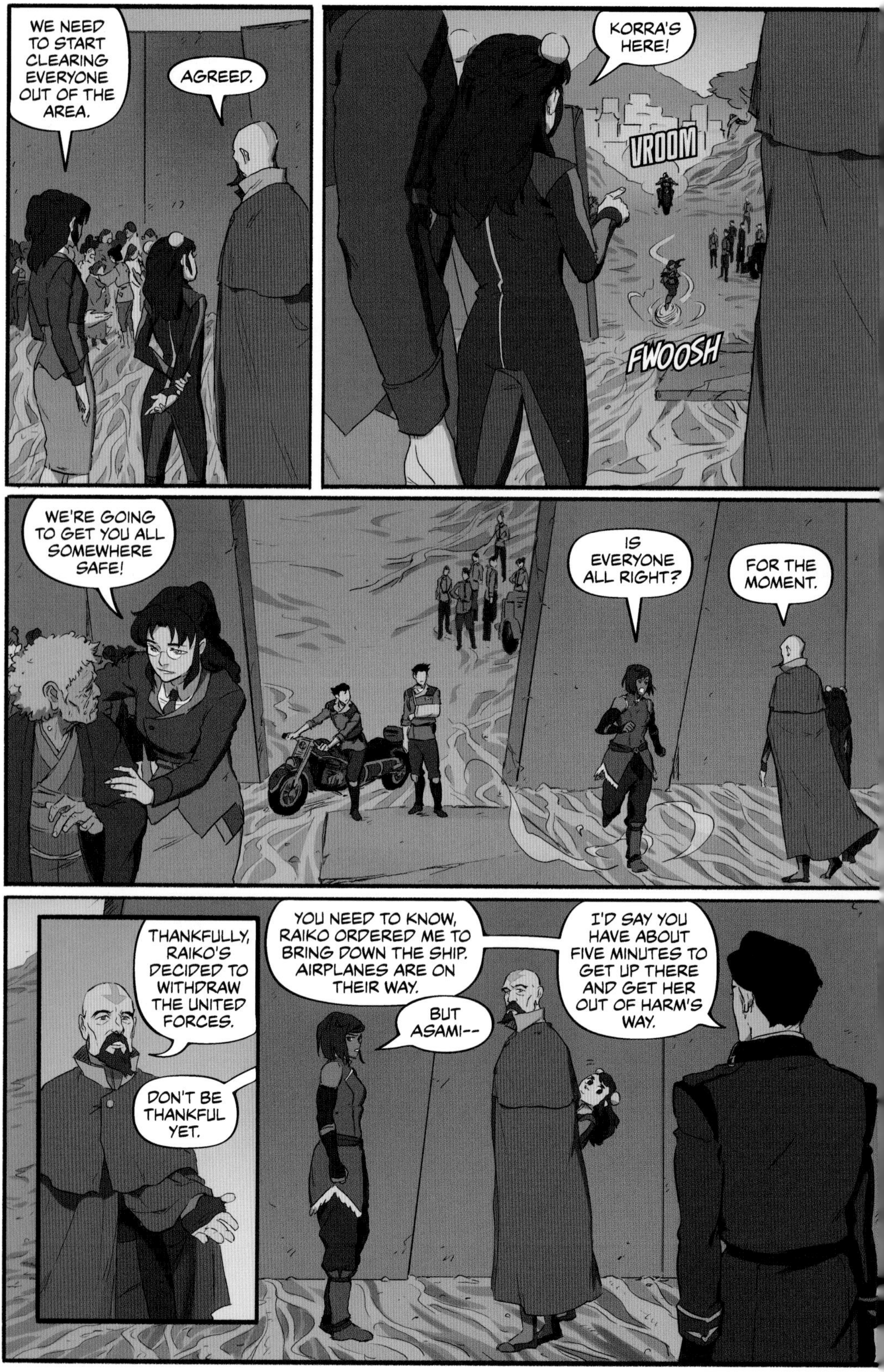
WE NEED TO START CLEARING EVERYONE OUT OF THE AREA.
AGREED.
KORRA'S HERE!
VROOM
FWOOSH
WE'RE GOING TO GET YOU ALL SOMEWHERE SAFE!
IS EVERYONE ALL RIGHT?
FOR THE MOMENT.
THANKFULLY, RAIKO'S DECIDED TO WITHDRAW THE UNITED FORCES.
DON'T BE THANKFUL YET.
YOU NEED TO KNOW, RAIKO ORDERED ME TO BRING DOWN THE SHIP. AIRPLANES ARE ON THEIR WAY.
BUT ASAMI--
I'D SAY YOU HAVE ABOUT FIVE MINUTES TO GET UP THERE AND GET HER OUT OF HARM'S WAY.

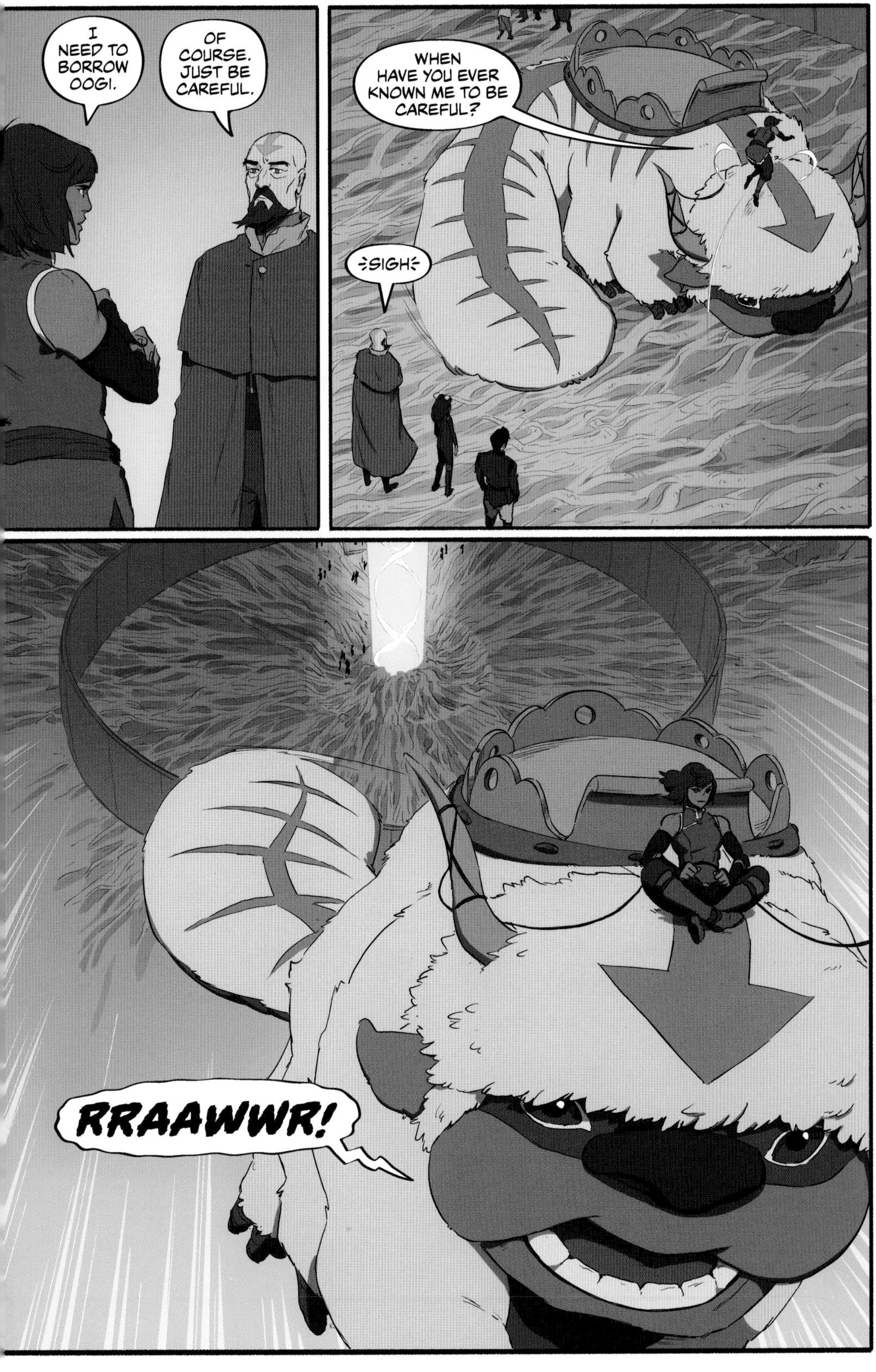
I NEED TO BORROW OOGI.
OF COURSE. JUST BE CAREFUL.
WHEN HAVE YOU EVER KNOWN ME TO BE CAREFUL?
SIGH
RRAAWWR!

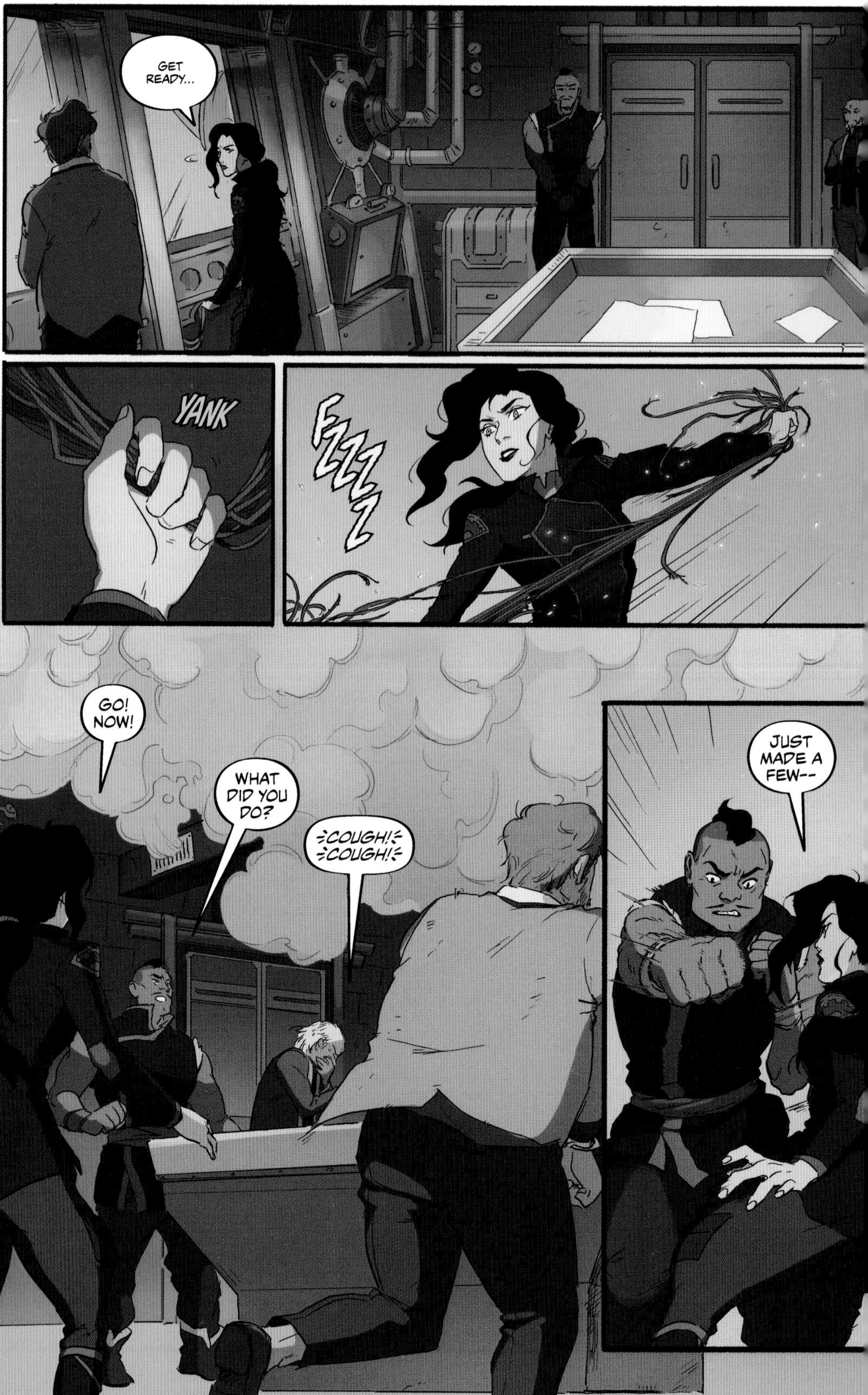
GET READY...
YANK
FZZZZ
GO! NOW!
WHAT DID YOU DO?
COUGH! COUGH!
JUST MADE A FEW--

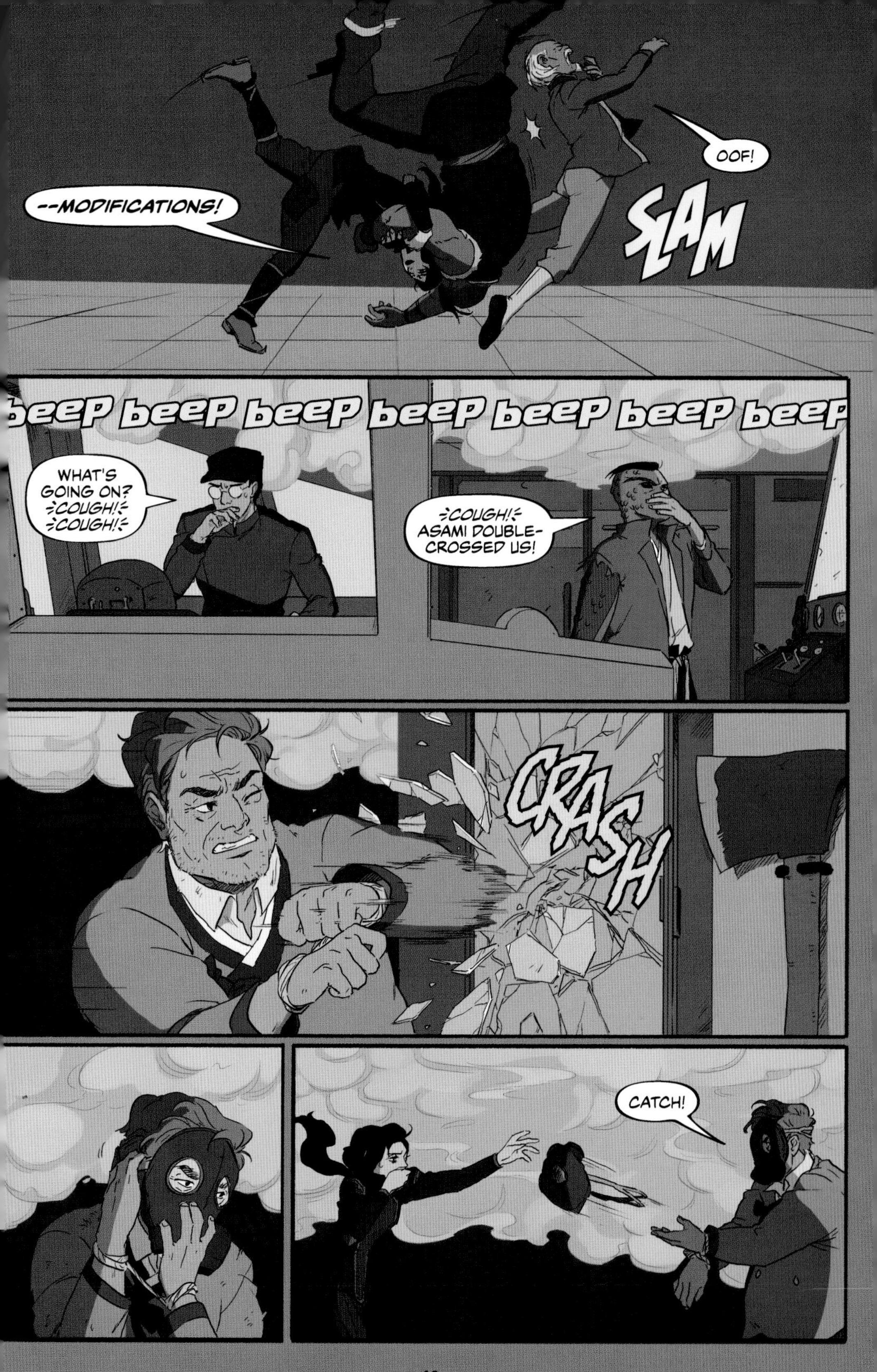
--MODIFICATIONS!
OOF!
SLAM
beep beep beep beep beep beep beep
WHAT'S GOING ON? COUGH! COUGH!
COUGH! ASAMI DOUBLE-CROSSED US!
CRASH
CATCH!

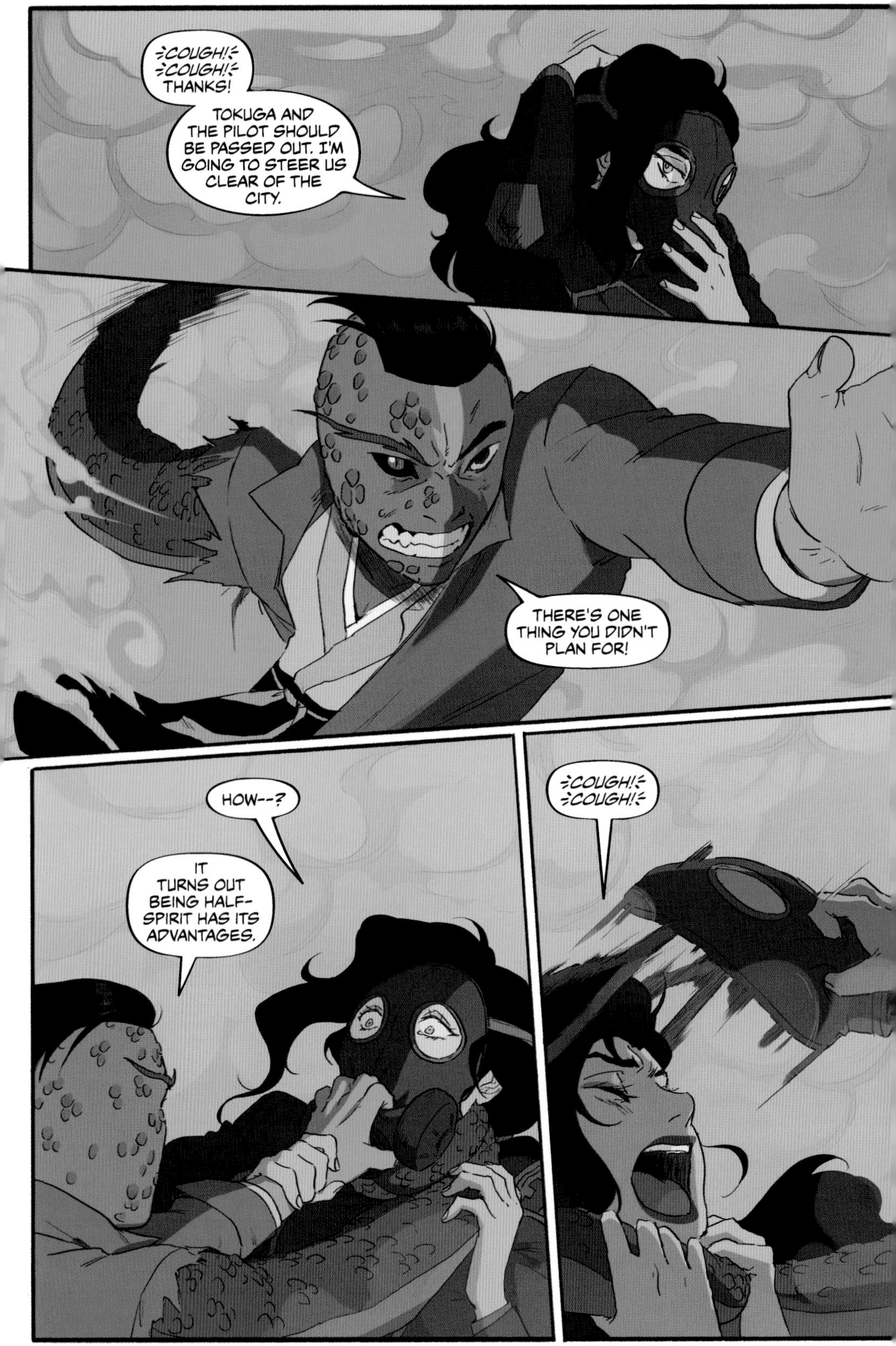

COUGH! COUGH! THANKS!
TOKUGA AND THE PILOT SHOULD BE PASSED OUT. I'M GOING TO STEER US CLEAR OF THE CITY.
THERE'S ONE THING YOU DIDN'T PLAN FOR!
HOW--?
IT TURNS OUT BEING HALF-SPIRIT HAS ITS ADVANTAGES.
COUGH! COUGH!

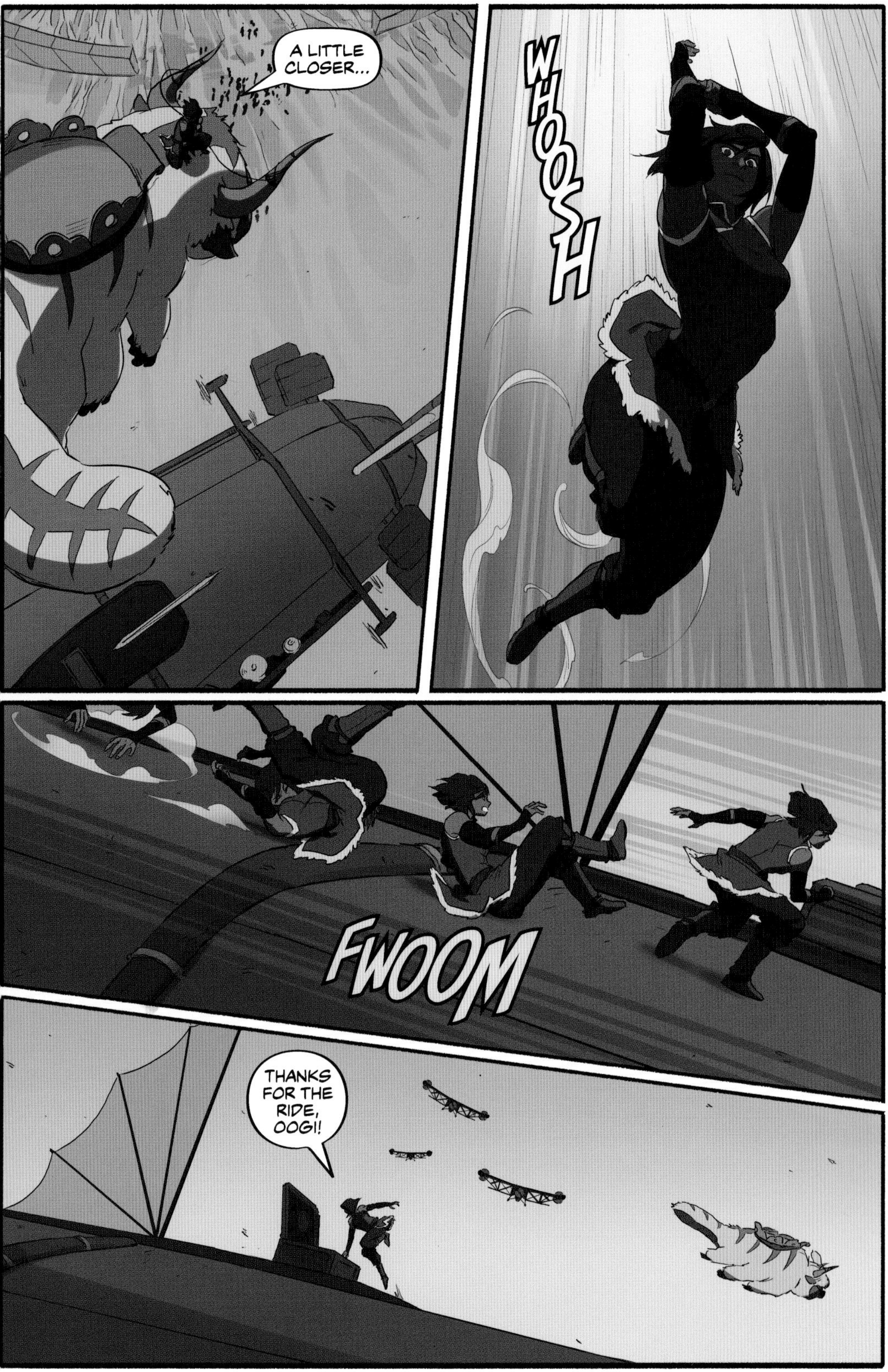
A LITTLE CLOSER...
WHOOSH
FWOOM
THANKS FOR THE RIDE, OOGI!

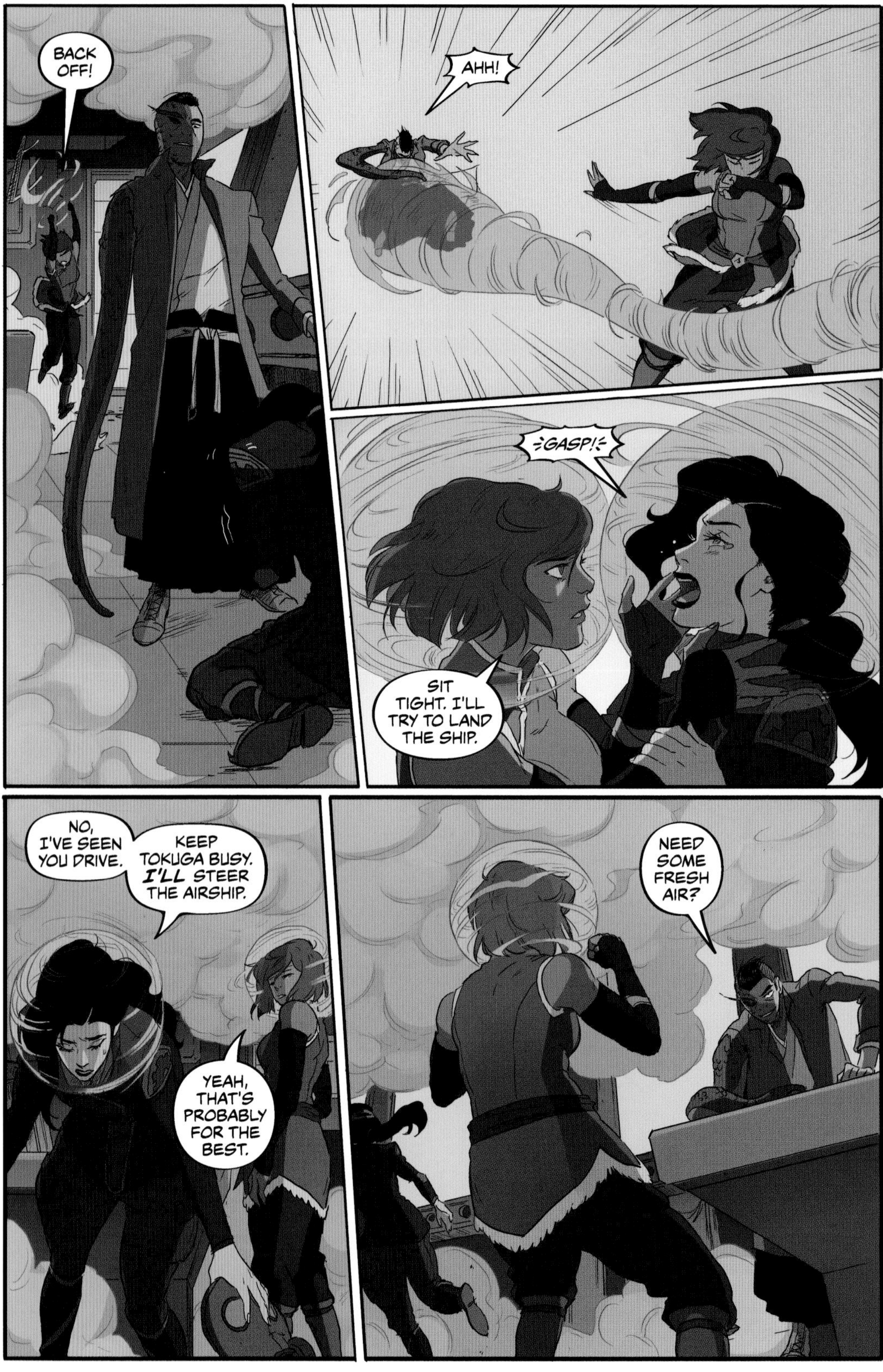
BACK OFF!
AHH!
GASP!
SIT TIGHT. I'LL TRY TO LAND THE SHIP.
NO, I'VE SEEN YOU DRIVE.
KEEP TOKUGA BUSY. I'LL STEER THE AIRSHIP.
YEAH, THAT'S PROBABLY FOR THE BEST.
NEED SOME FRESH AIR?

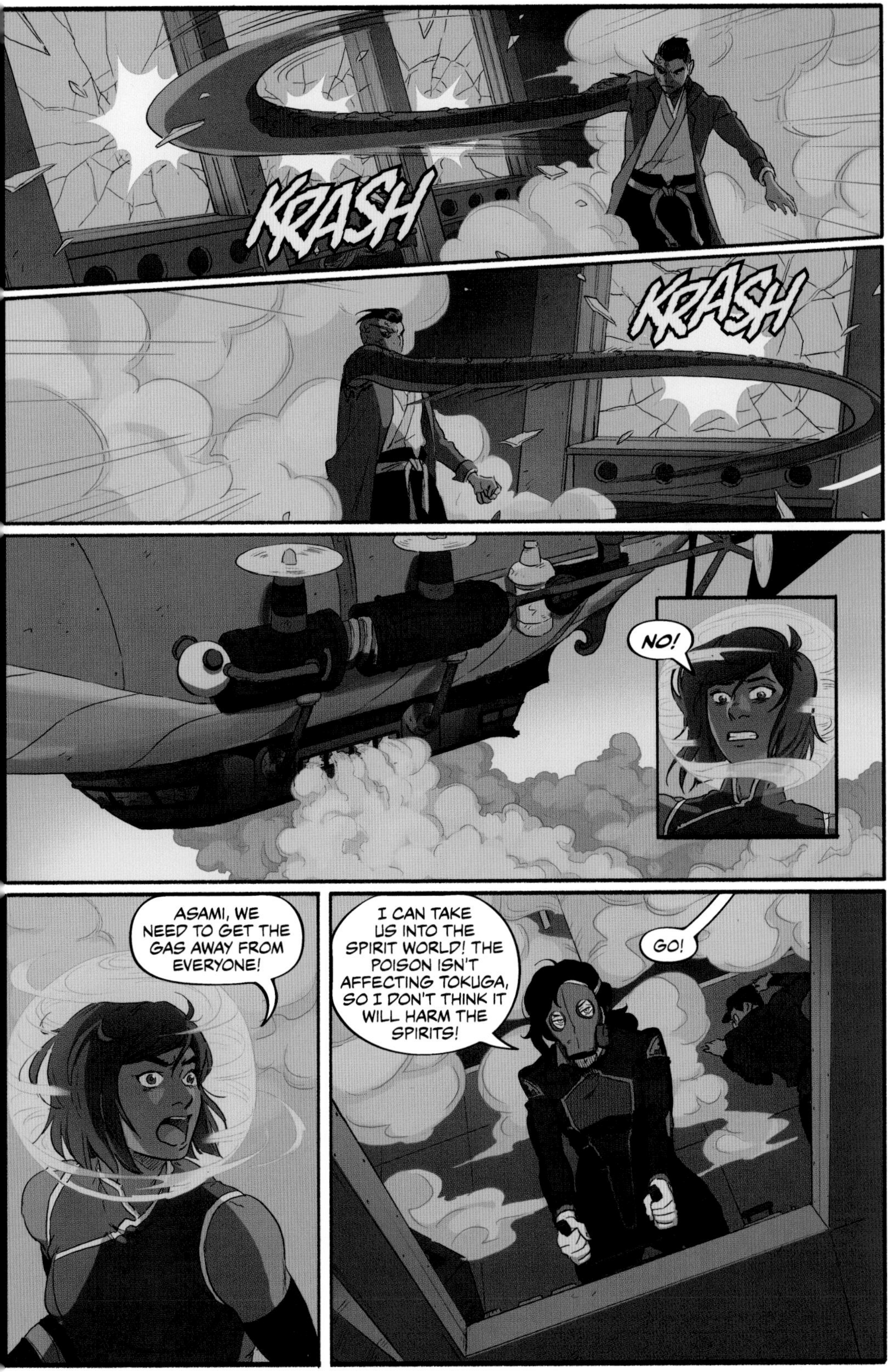
KRASH
KRASH
NO!
ASAMI, WE NEED TO GET THE GAS AWAY FROM EVERYONE!
I CAN TAKE US INTO THE SPIRIT WORLD! THE POISON ISN'T AFFECTING TOKUGA, SO I DON'T THINK IT WILL HARM THE SPIRITS!
GO!

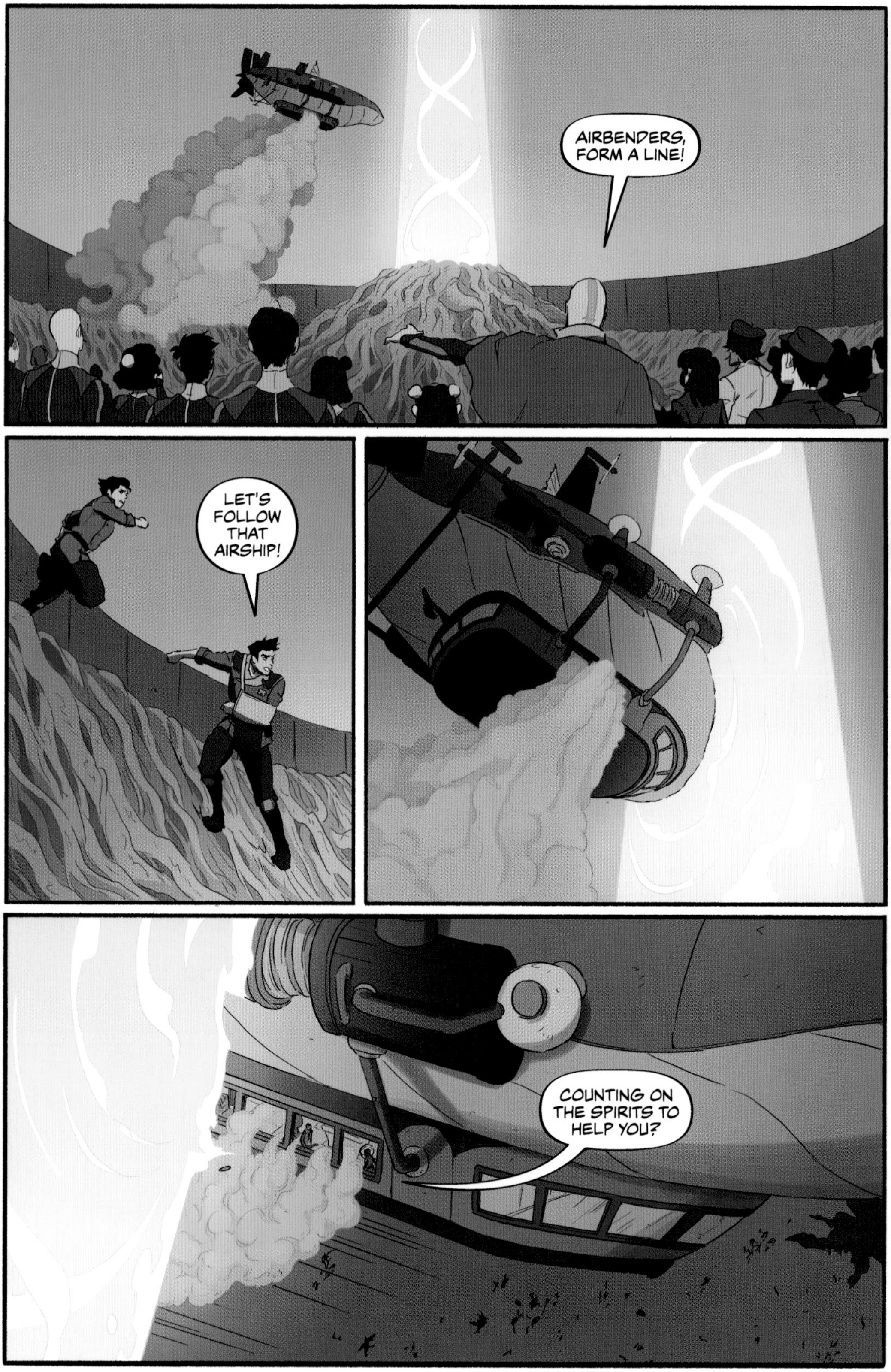
AIRBENDERS, FORM A LINE!
LET'S FOLLOW THAT AIRSHIP!
COUNTING ON THE SPIRITS TO HELP YOU?

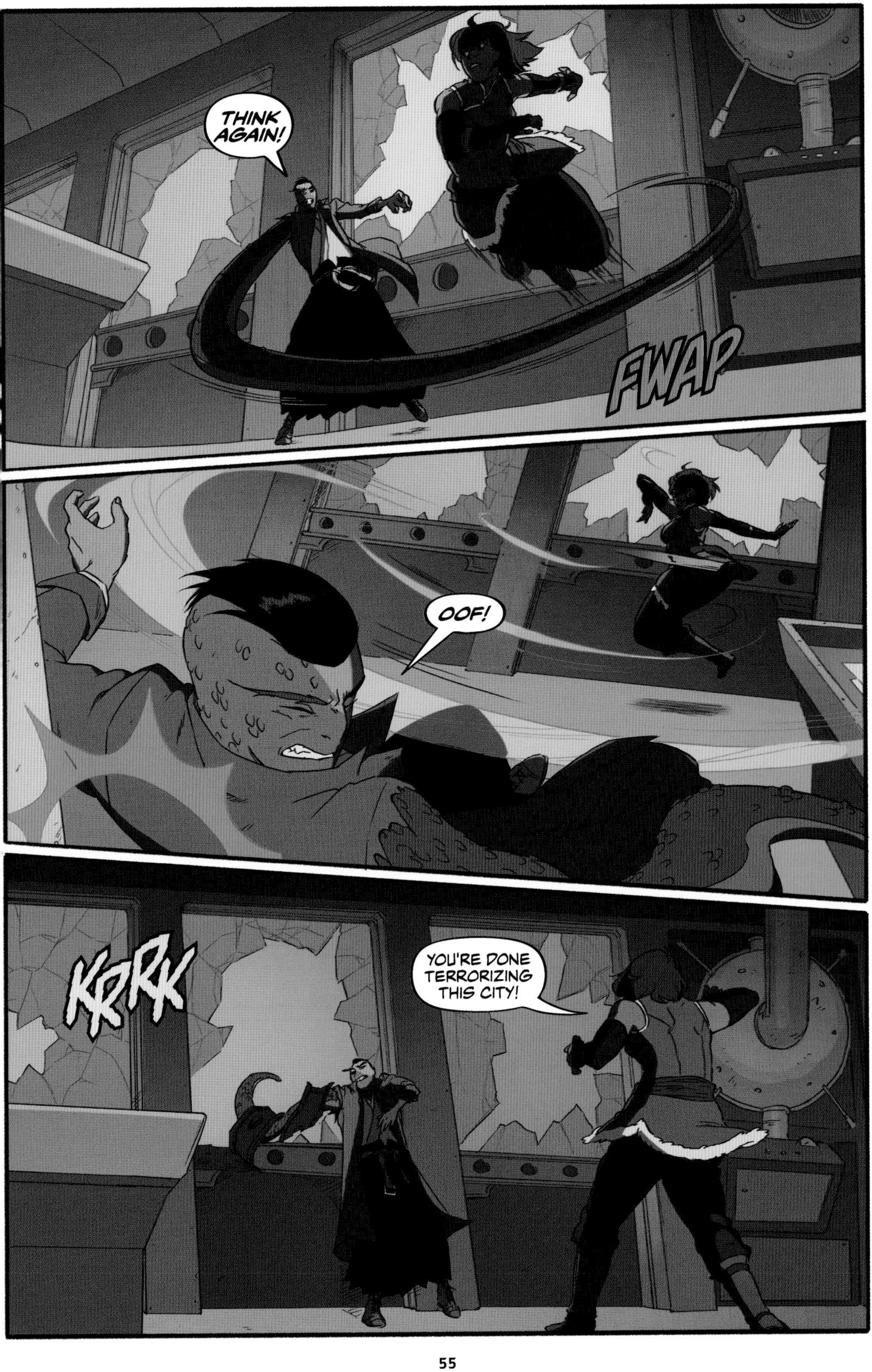
THINK AGAIN!
FWAP
OOF!
KRRK
YOU'RE DONE TERRORIZING THIS CITY!

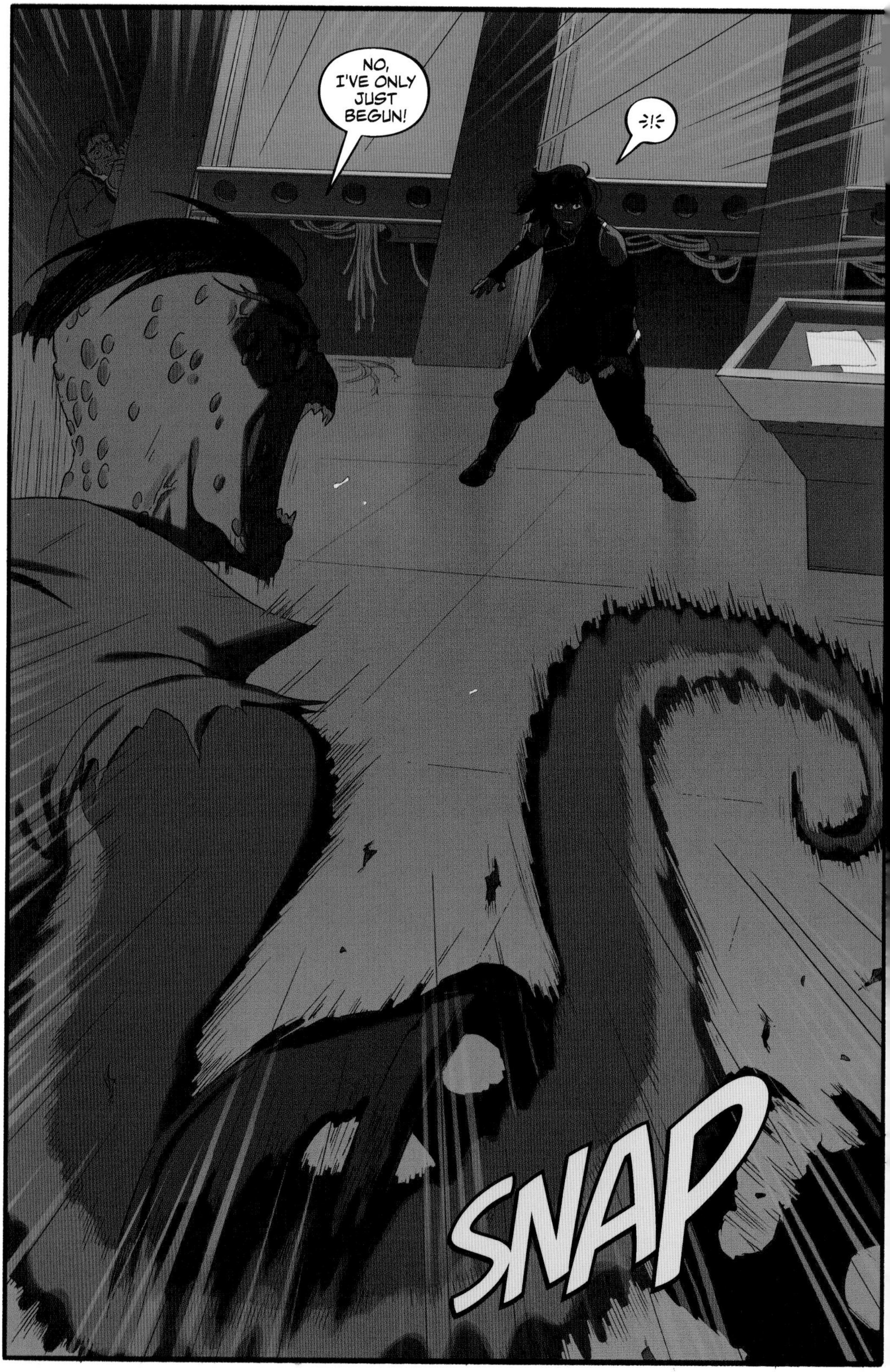
NO, I'VE ONLY JUST BEGUN!
!
SNAP

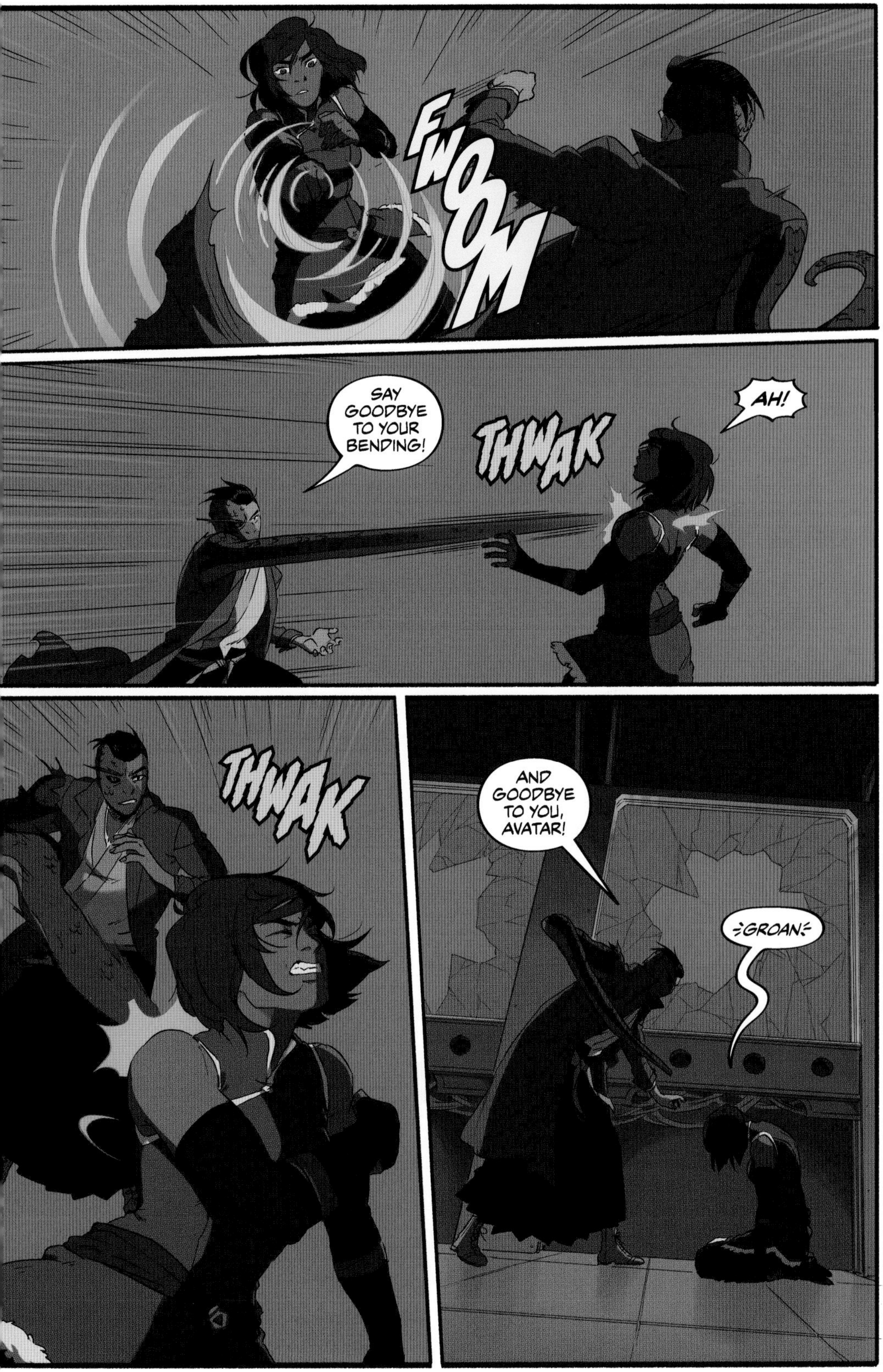
FWOOM
SAY GOODBYE TO YOUR BENDING!
THWAK
AH!
THWAK
AND GOODBYE TO YOU, AVATAR!
GROAN

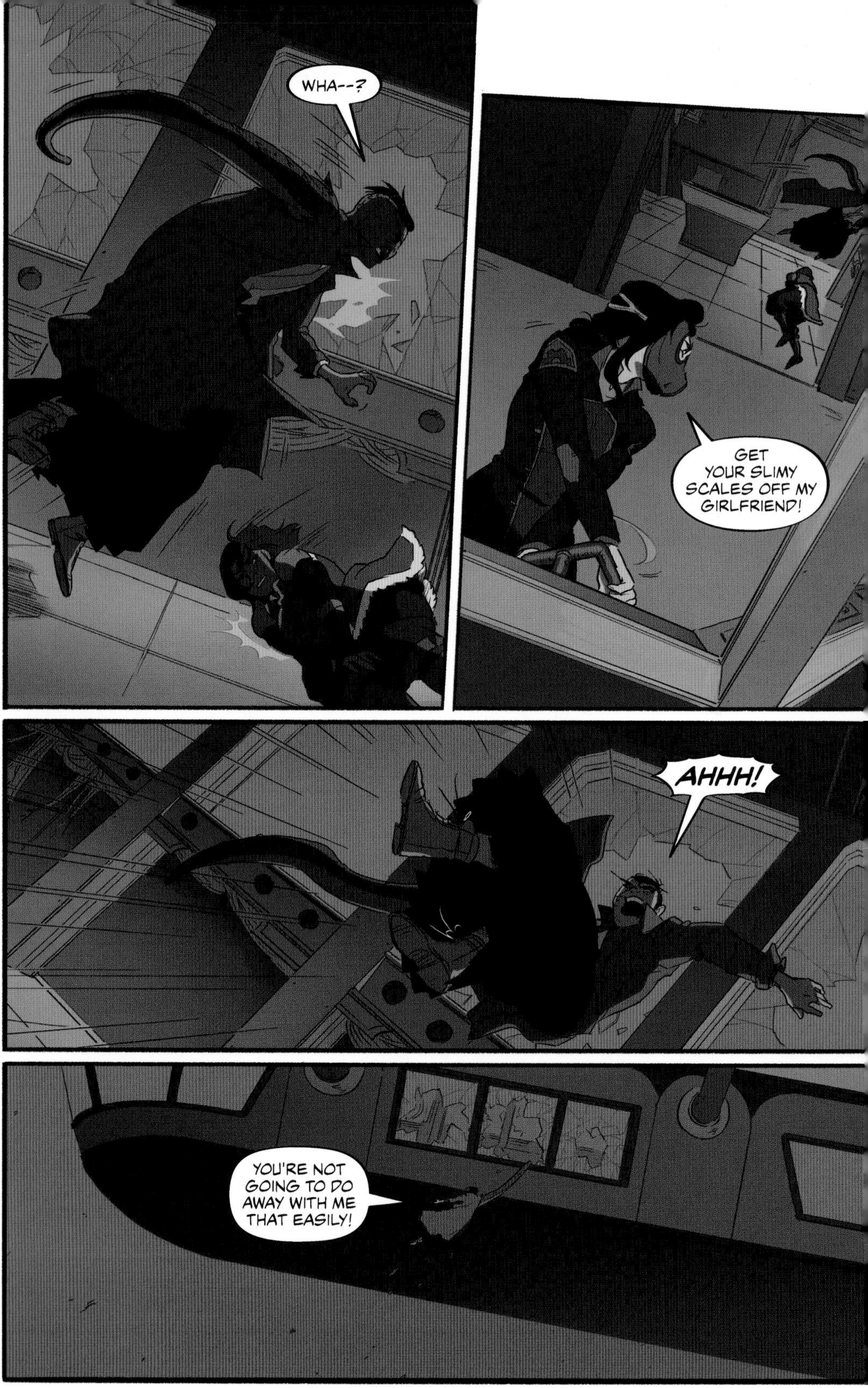
WHA--?
GET YOUR SLIMY SCALES OFF MY GIRLFRIEND!
AHHH!
YOU'RE NOT GOING TO DO AWAY WITH ME THAT EASILY!

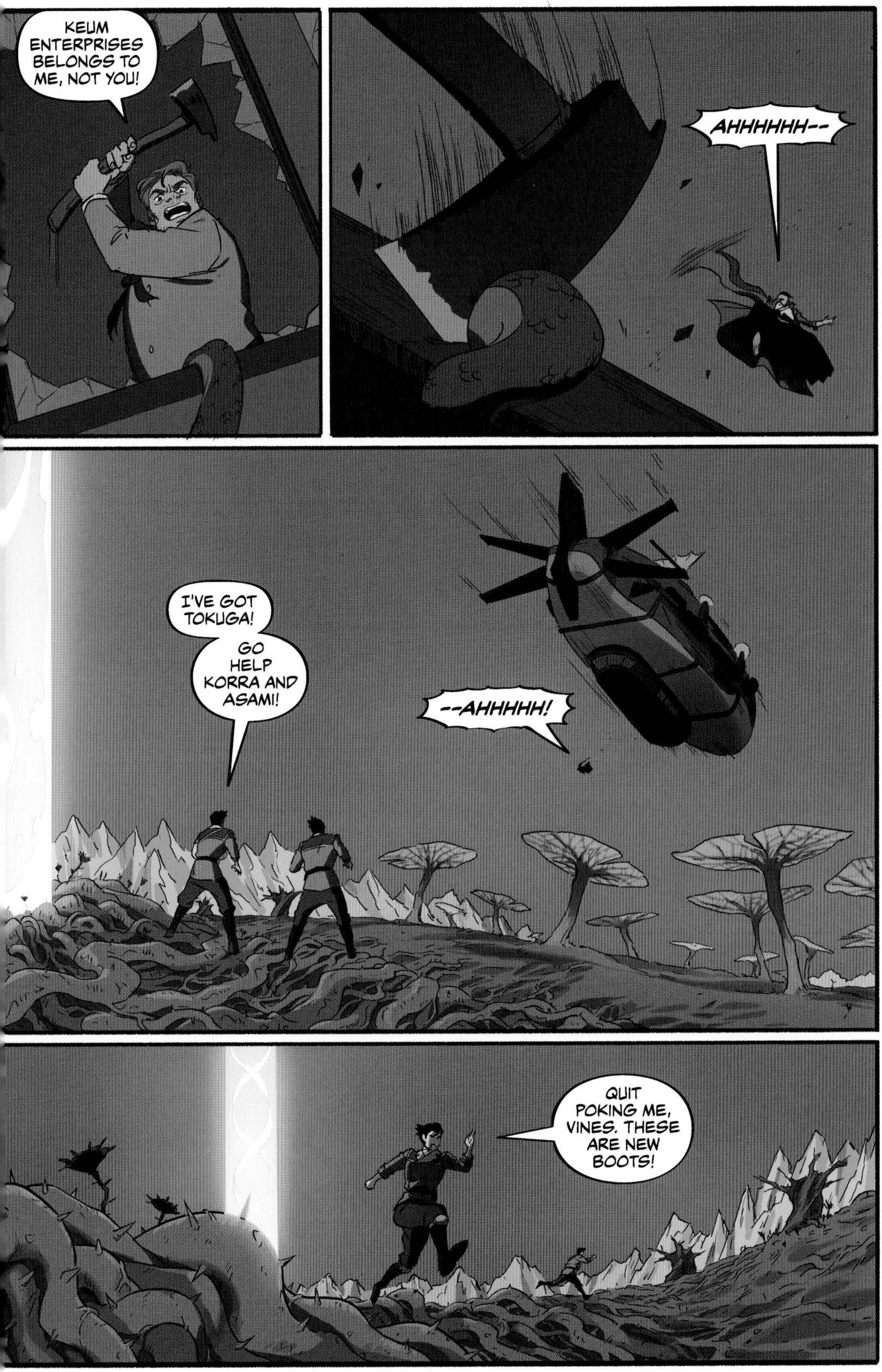
KEUM ENTERPRISES BELONGS TO ME, NOT YOU!
AHHHHHH--
I'VE GOT TOKUGA!
GO HELP KORRA AND ASAMI!
--AHHHHH!
QUIT POKING ME, VINES. THESE ARE NEW BOOTS!

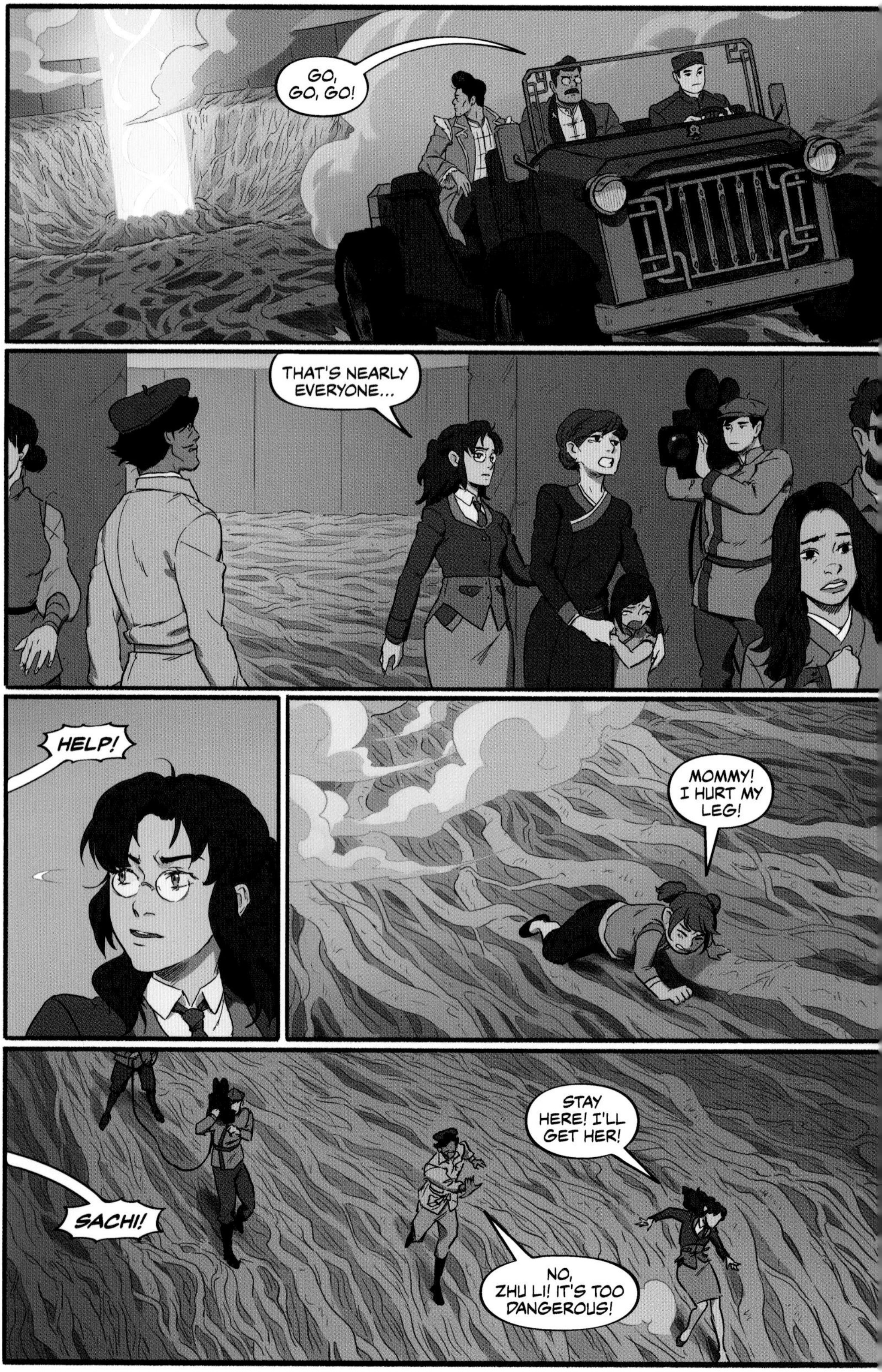
GO, GO, GO!
THAT'S NEARLY EVERYONE...
HELP!
MOMMY! I HURT MY LEG!
SACHI!
STAY HERE! I'LL GET HER!
NO, ZHU LI! IT'S TOO DANGEROUS!

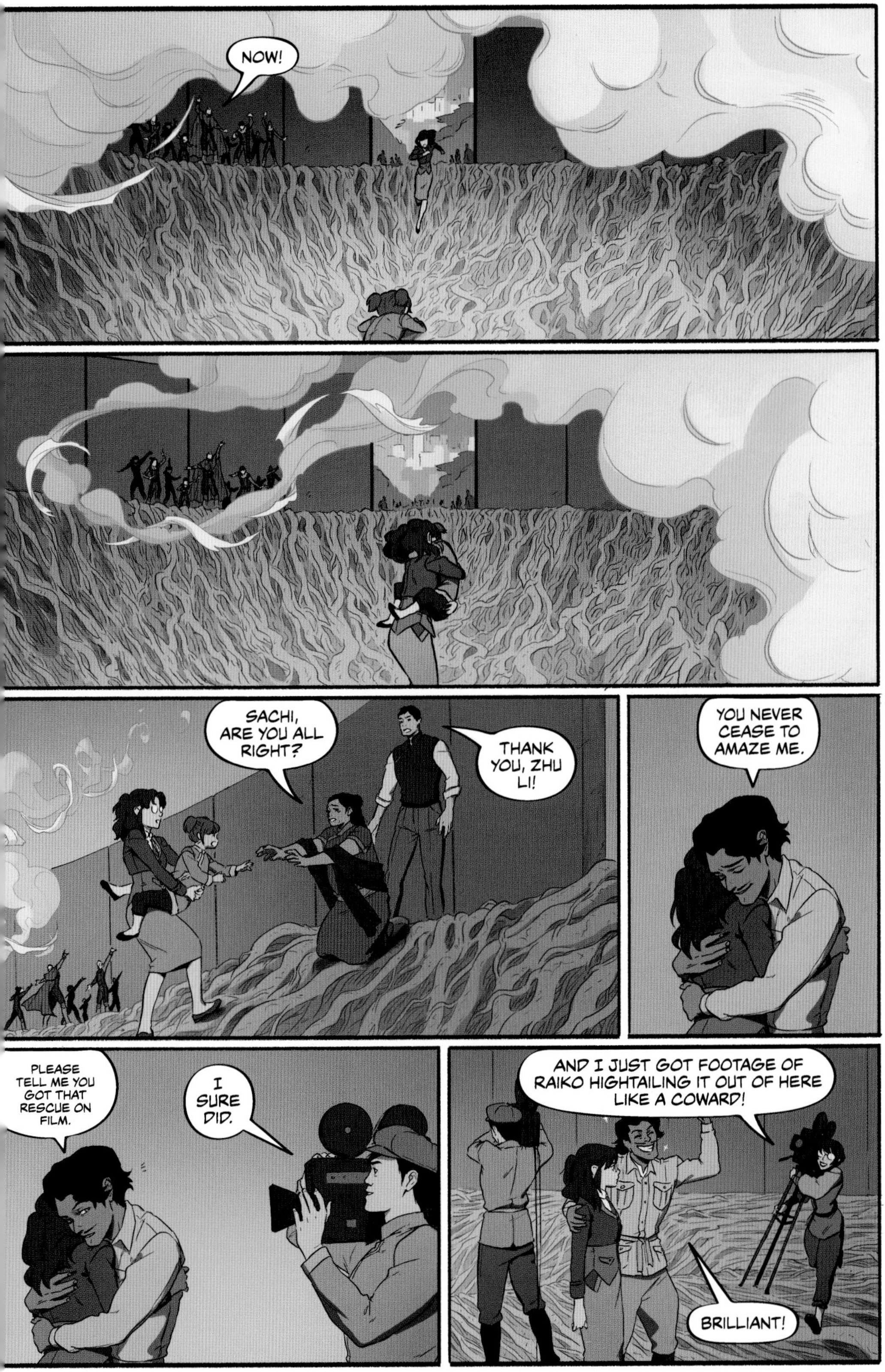
NOW!
SACHI, ARE YOU ALL RIGHT?
THANK YOU, ZHU LI!
YOU NEVER CEASE TO AMAZE ME.
PLEASE TELL ME YOU GOT THAT RESCUE ON FILM.
I SURE DID.
AND I JUST GOT FOOTAGE OF RAIKO HIGHTAILING IT OUT OF HERE LIKE A COWARD!
BRILLIANT!

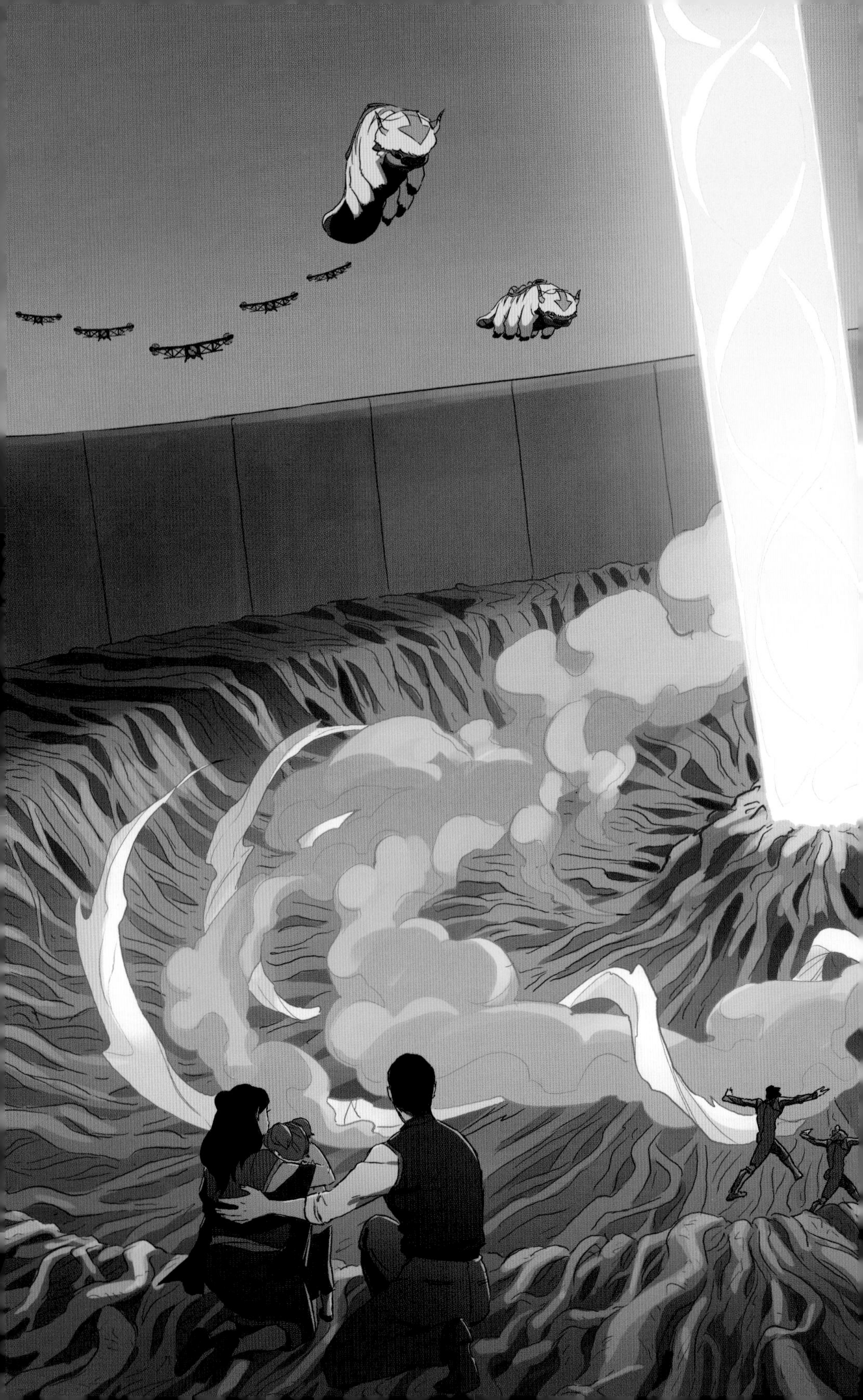

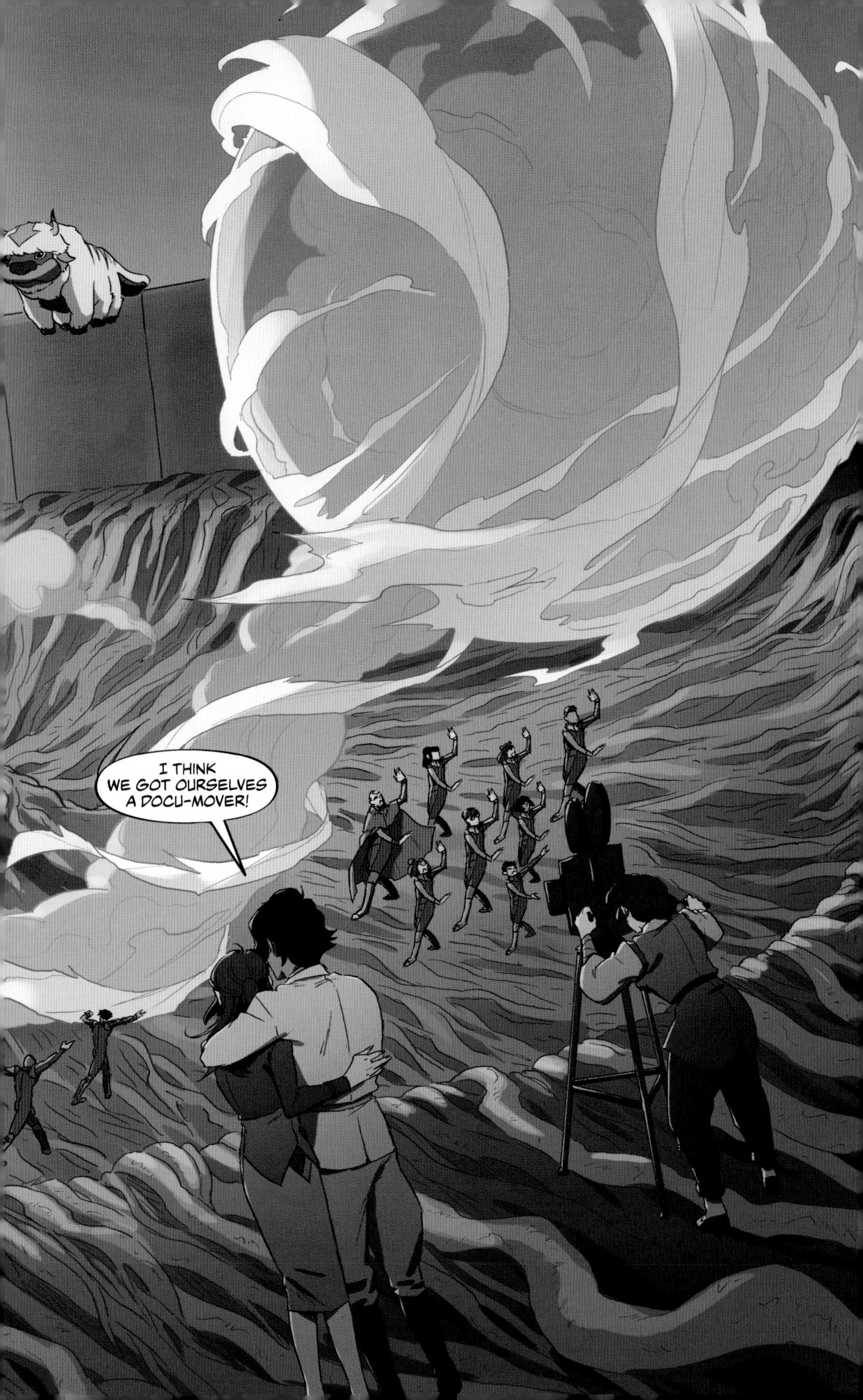
I THINK WE GOT OURSELVES A DOCU-MOVER!

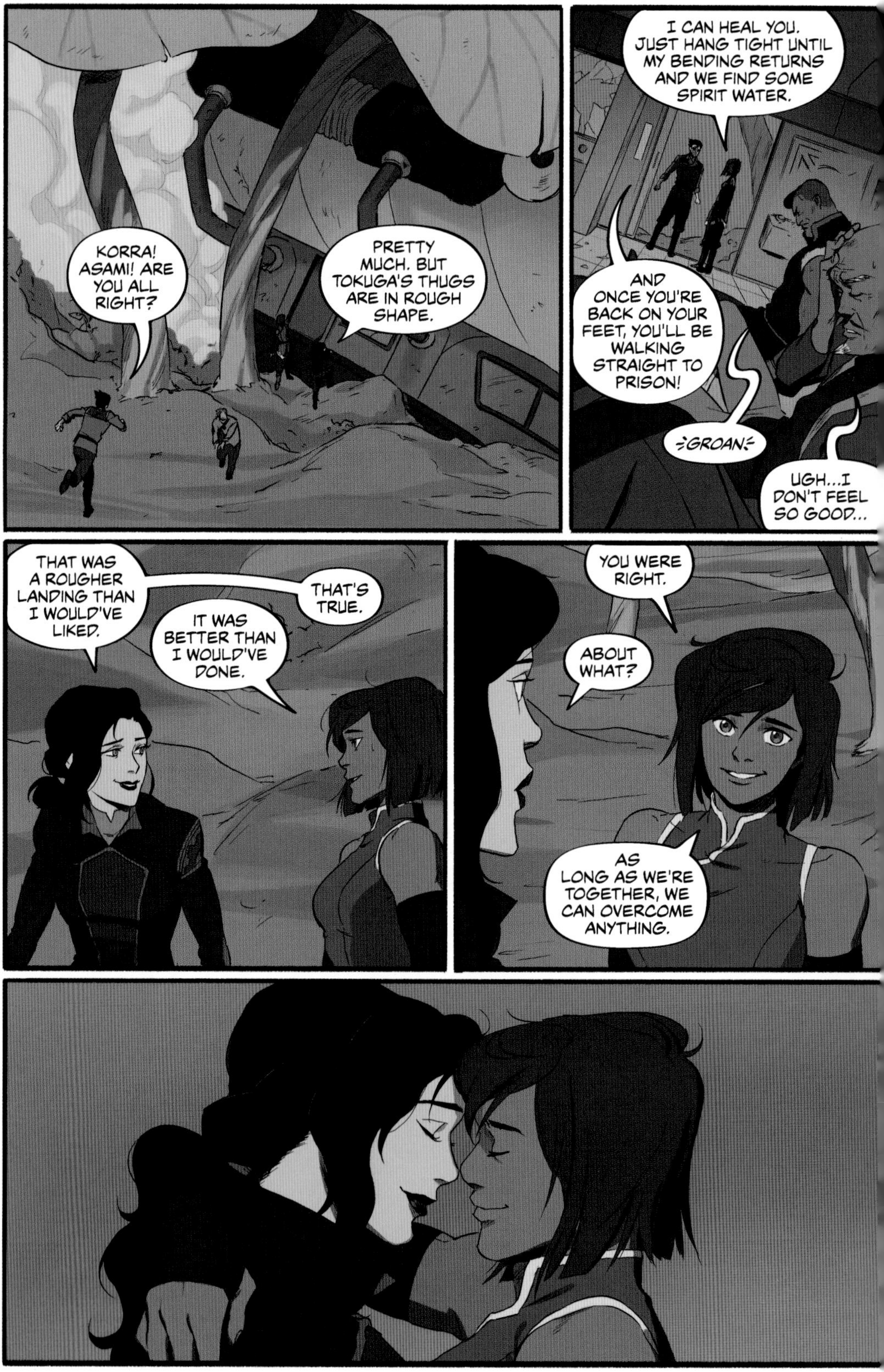
KORRA! ASAMI! ARE YOU ALL RIGHT?
PRETTY MUCH. BUT TOKUGA'S THUGS ARE IN ROUGH SHAPE.
I CAN HEAL YOU. JUST HANG TIGHT UNTIL MY BENDING RETURNS AND WE FIND SOME SPIRIT WATER.
AND ONCE YOU'RE BACK ON YOUR FEET, YOU'LL BE WALKING STRAIGHT TO PRISON!
GROAN
UGH...I DON'T FEEL SO GOOD...
THAT WAS A ROUGHER LANDING THAN I WOULD'VE LIKED.
IT WAS BETTER THAN I WOULD'VE DONE.
THAT'S TRUE.
YOU WERE RIGHT.
ABOUT WHAT?
AS LONG AS WE'RE TOGETHER, WE CAN OVERCOME ANYTHING.

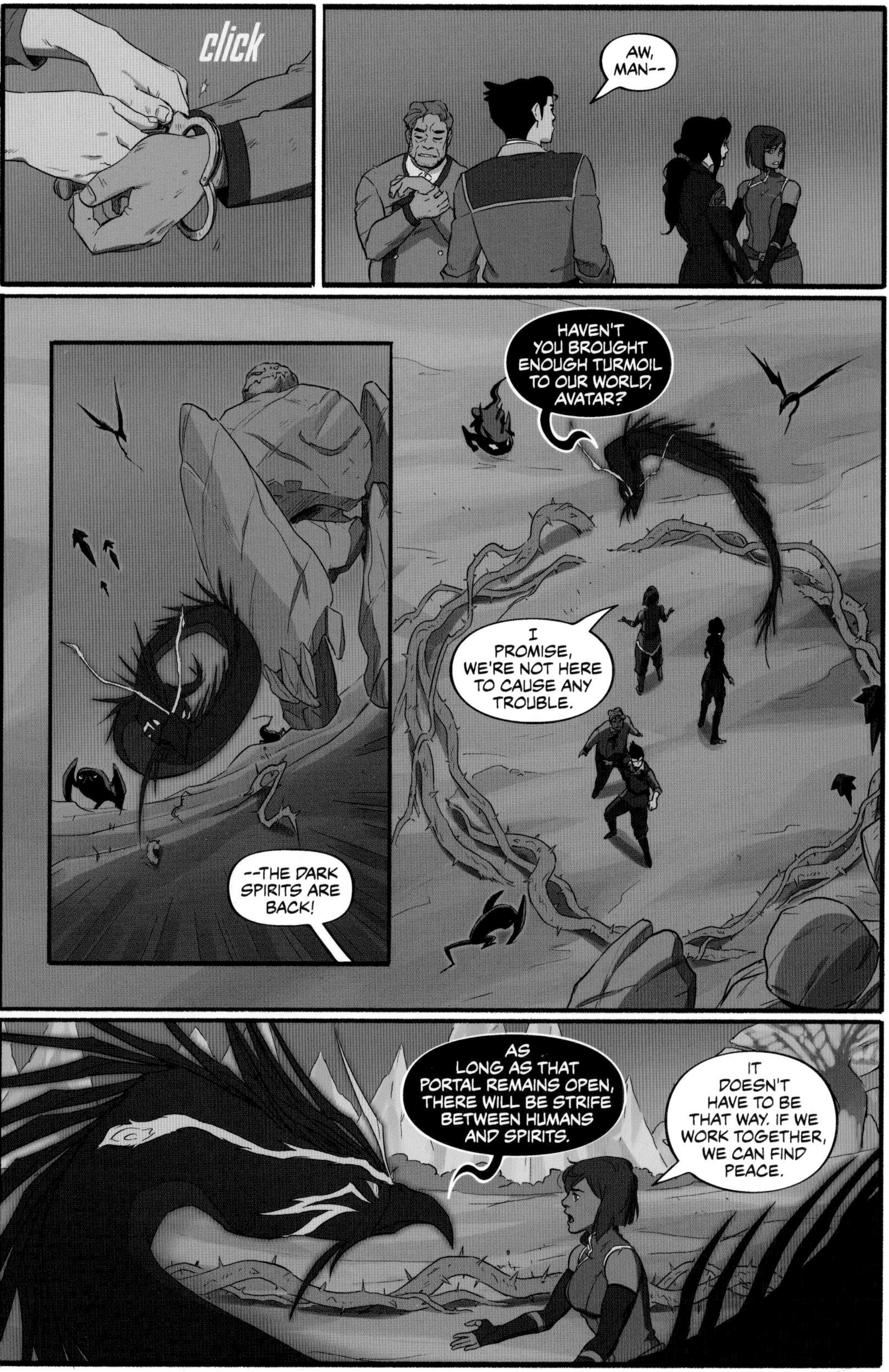
click
AW, MAN--
HAVEN'T YOU BROUGHT ENOUGH TURMOIL TO OUR WORLD, AVATAR?
--THE DARK SPIRITS ARE BACK!
I PROMISE, WE'RE NOT HERE TO CAUSE ANY TROUBLE.
AS LONG AS THAT PORTAL REMAINS OPEN, THERE WILL BE STRIFE BETWEEN HUMANS AND SPIRITS.
IT DOESN'T HAVE TO BE THAT WAY. IF WE WORK TOGETHER, WE CAN FIND PEACE.

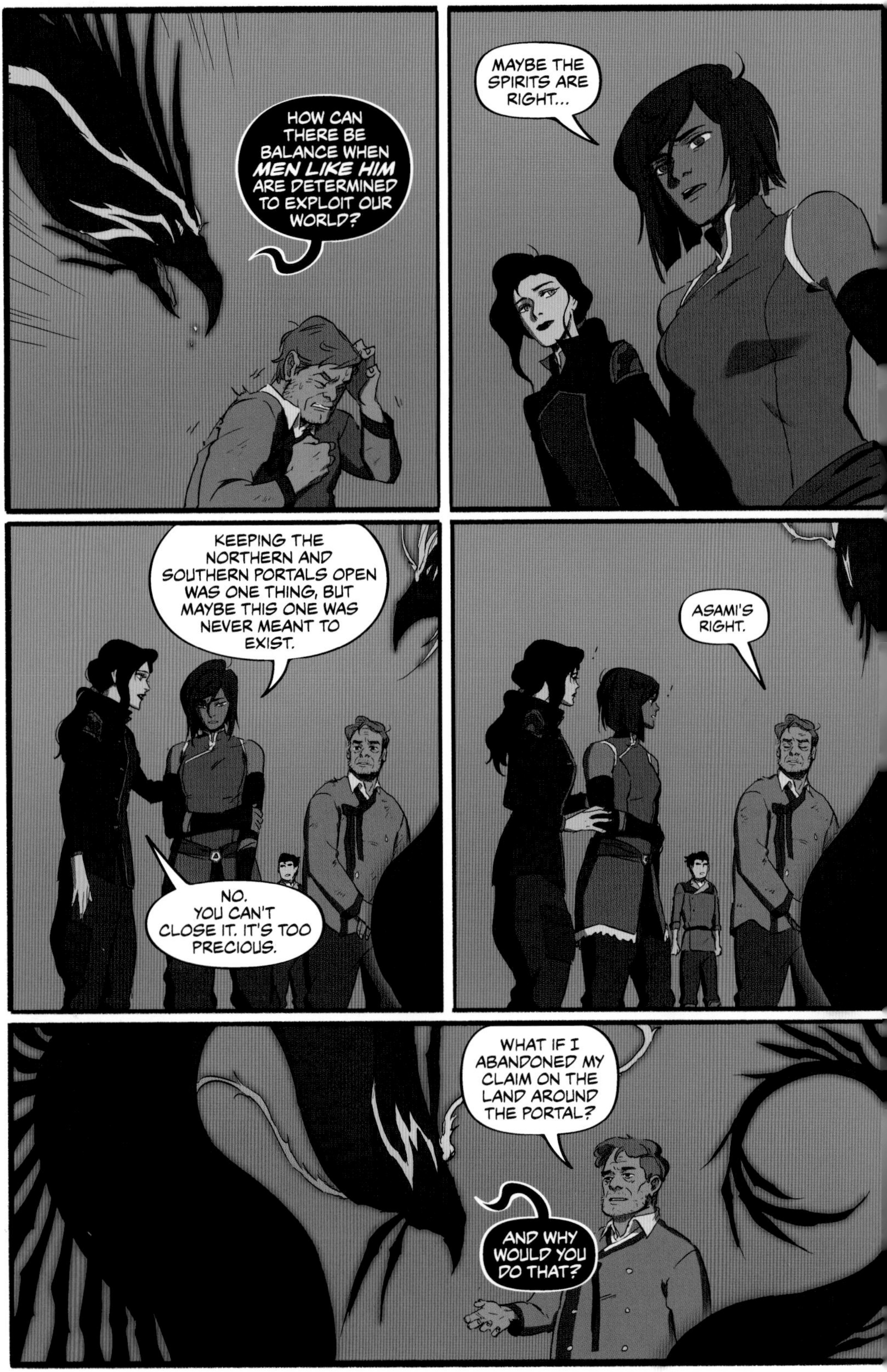
HOW CAN THERE BE BALANCE WHEN ***MEN LIKE HIM*** ARE DETERMINED TO EXPLOIT OUR WORLD?
MAYBE THE SPIRITS ARE RIGHT...
KEEPING THE NORTHERN AND SOUTHERN PORTALS OPEN WAS ONE THING, BUT MAYBE THIS ONE WAS NEVER MEANT TO EXIST.
NO. YOU CAN'T CLOSE IT. IT'S TOO PRECIOUS.
ASAMI'S RIGHT.
WHAT IF I ABANDONED MY CLAIM ON THE LAND AROUND THE PORTAL?
AND WHY WOULD YOU DO THAT?

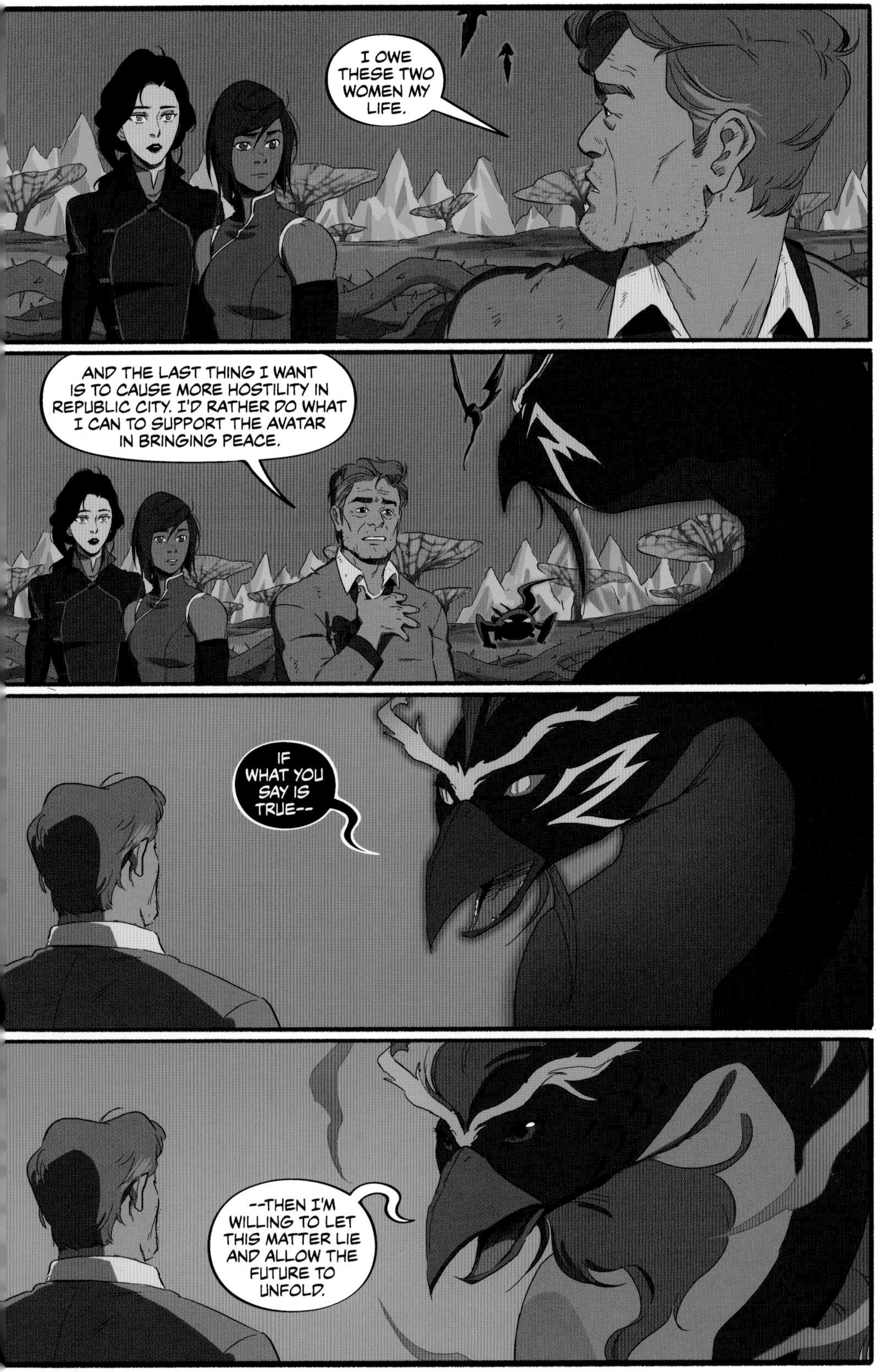
I OWE THESE TWO WOMEN MY LIFE.
AND THE LAST THING I WANT IS TO CAUSE MORE HOSTILITY IN REPUBLIC CITY. I'D RATHER DO WHAT I CAN TO SUPPORT THE AVATAR IN BRINGING PEACE.
IF WHAT YOU SAY IS TRUE--
--THEN I'M WILLING TO LET THIS MATTER LIE AND ALLOW THE FUTURE TO UNFOLD.

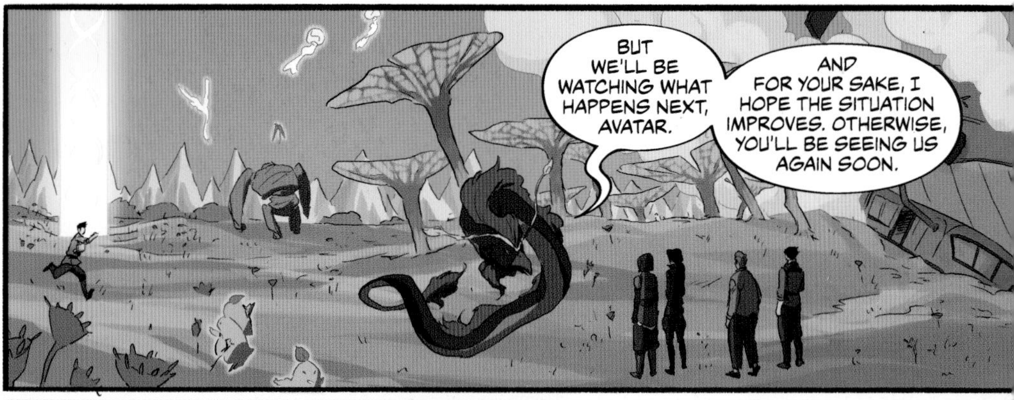
BUT WE'LL BE WATCHING WHAT HAPPENS NEXT, AVATAR.
AND FOR YOUR SAKE, I HOPE THE SITUATION IMPROVES. OTHERWISE, YOU'LL BE SEEING US AGAIN SOON.

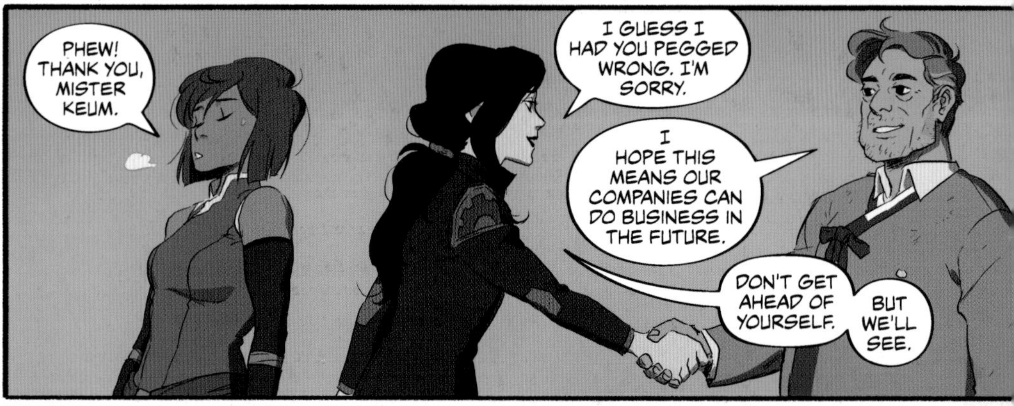
PHEW! THANK YOU, MISTER KEUM.
I GUESS I HAD YOU PEGGED WRONG. I'M SORRY.
I HOPE THIS MEANS OUR COMPANIES CAN DO BUSINESS IN THE FUTURE.
DON'T GET AHEAD OF YOURSELF.
BUT WE'LL SEE.

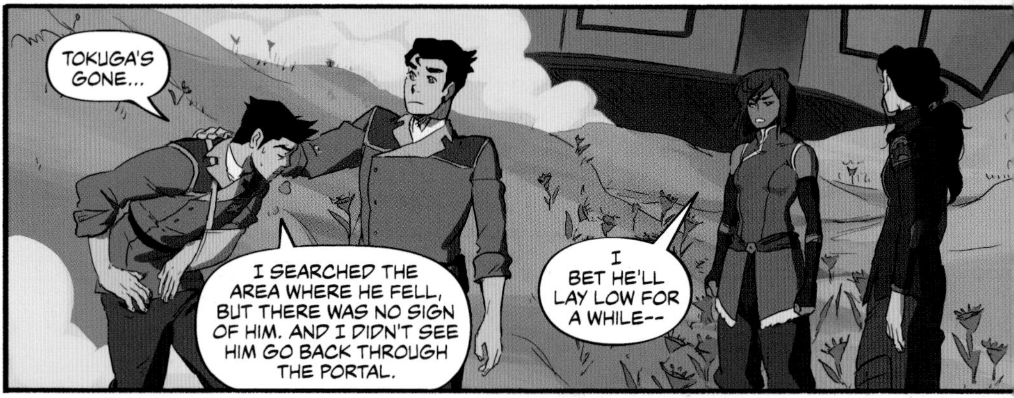
TOKUGA'S GONE...
I SEARCHED THE AREA WHERE HE FELL, BUT THERE WAS NO SIGN OF HIM. AND I DIDN'T SEE HIM GO BACK THROUGH THE PORTAL.
I BET HE'LL LAY LOW FOR A WHILE--

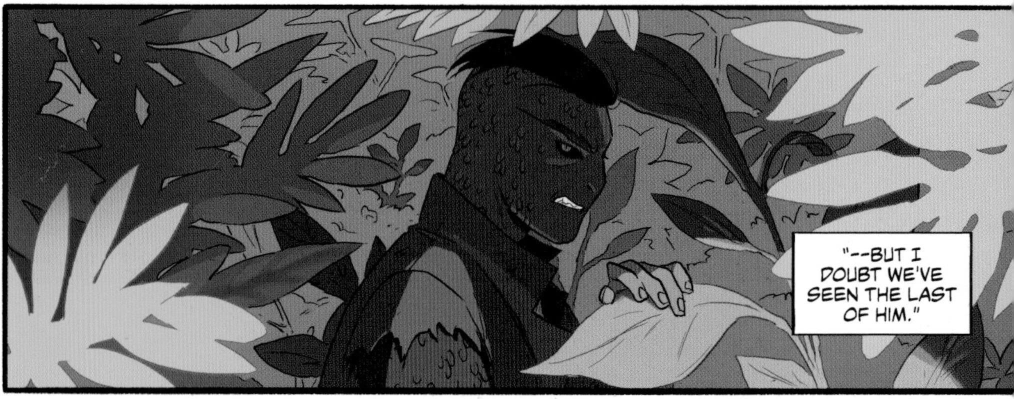
"--BUT I DOUBT WE'VE SEEN THE LAST OF HIM."

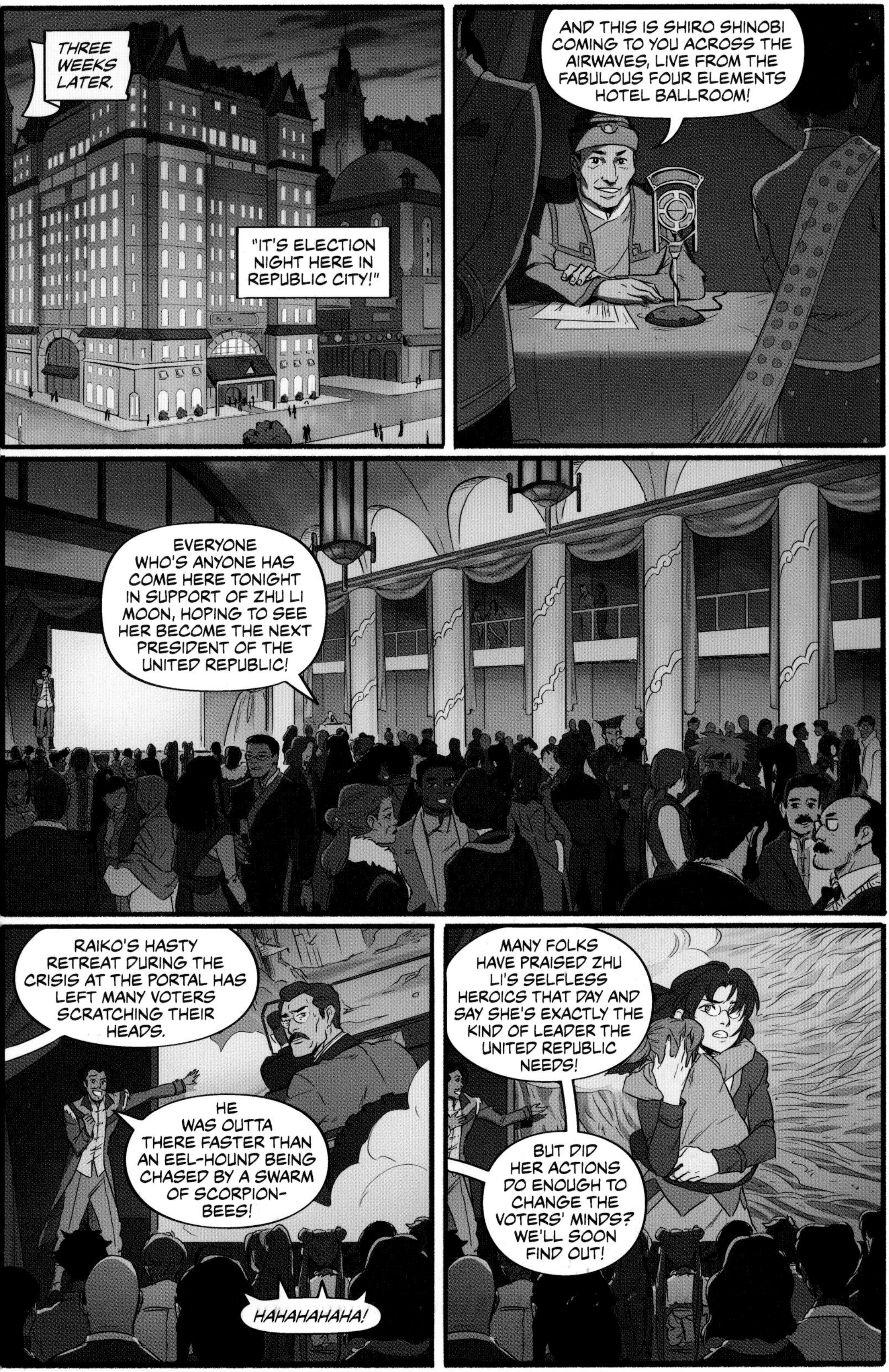
THREE WEEKS LATER.
"IT'S ELECTION NIGHT HERE IN REPUBLIC CITY!"
AND THIS IS SHIRO SHINOBI COMING TO YOU ACROSS THE AIRWAVES, LIVE FROM THE FABULOUS FOUR ELEMENTS HOTEL BALLROOM!
EVERYONE WHO'S ANYONE HAS COME HERE TONIGHT IN SUPPORT OF ZHU LI MOON, HOPING TO SEE HER BECOME THE NEXT PRESIDENT OF THE UNITED REPUBLIC!
RAIKO'S HASTY RETREAT DURING THE CRISIS AT THE PORTAL HAS LEFT MANY VOTERS SCRATCHING THEIR HEADS.
HE WAS OUTTA THERE FASTER THAN AN EEL-HOUND BEING CHASED BY A SWARM OF SCORPION-BEES!
HAHAHAHAHA!
MANY FOLKS HAVE PRAISED ZHU LI'S SELFLESS HEROICS THAT DAY AND SAY SHE'S EXACTLY THE KIND OF LEADER THE UNITED REPUBLIC NEEDS!
BUT DID HER ACTIONS DO ENOUGH TO CHANGE THE VOTERS' MINDS? WE'LL SOON FIND OUT!

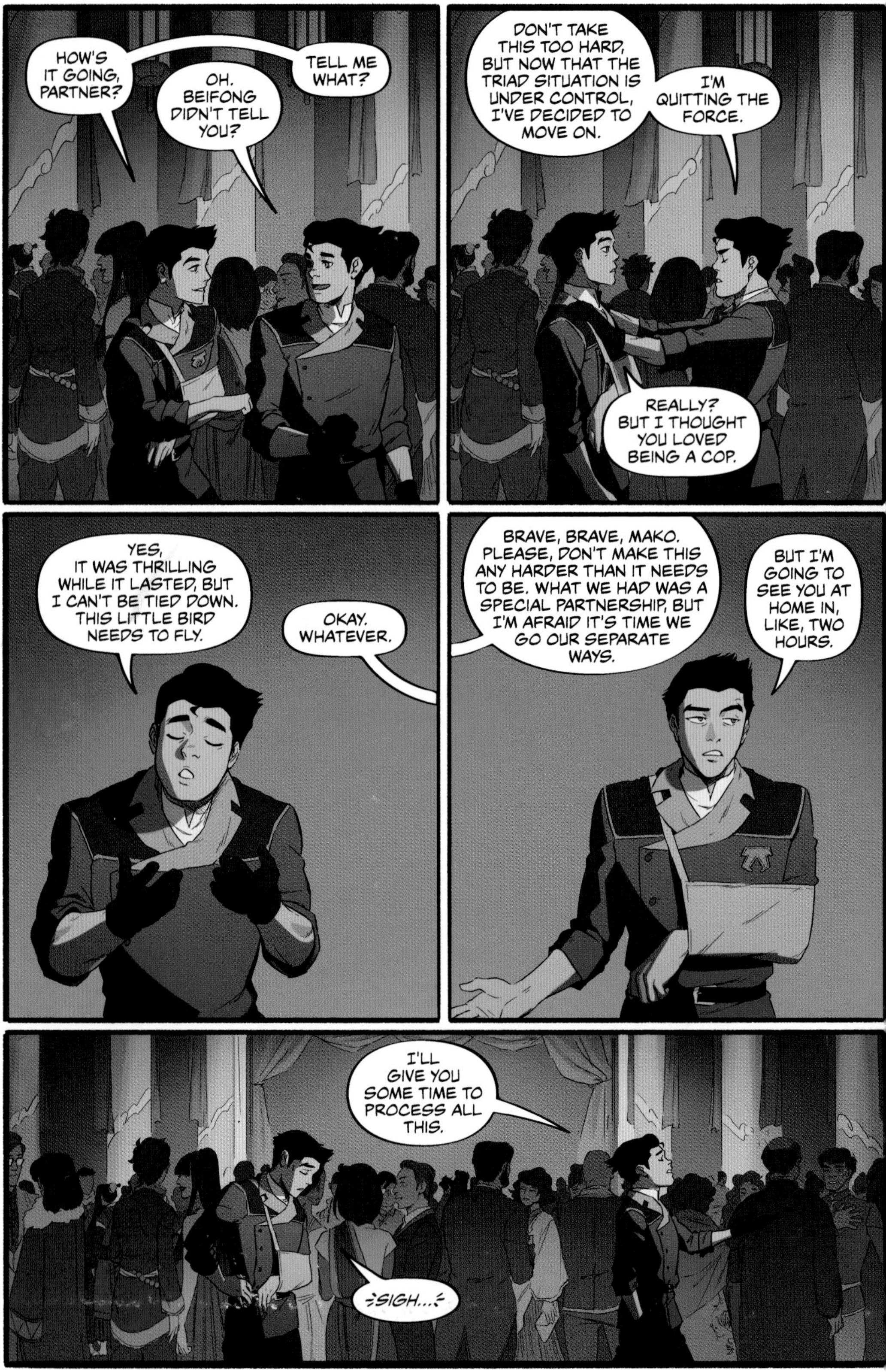
HOW'S IT GOING, PARTNER?
OH. BEIFONG DIDN'T TELL YOU?
TELL ME WHAT?
DON'T TAKE THIS TOO HARD, BUT NOW THAT THE TRIAD SITUATION IS UNDER CONTROL, I'VE DECIDED TO MOVE ON.
I'M QUITTING THE FORCE.
REALLY? BUT I THOUGHT YOU LOVED BEING A COP.
YES, IT WAS THRILLING WHILE IT LASTED, BUT I CAN'T BE TIED DOWN. THIS LITTLE BIRD NEEDS TO FLY.
OKAY. WHATEVER.
BRAVE, BRAVE, MAKO. PLEASE, DON'T MAKE THIS ANY HARDER THAN IT NEEDS TO BE. WHAT WE HAD WAS A SPECIAL PARTNERSHIP, BUT I'M AFRAID IT'S TIME WE GO OUR SEPARATE WAYS.
BUT I'M GOING TO SEE YOU AT HOME IN, LIKE, TWO HOURS.
I'LL GIVE YOU SOME TIME TO PROCESS ALL THIS.
SIGH...

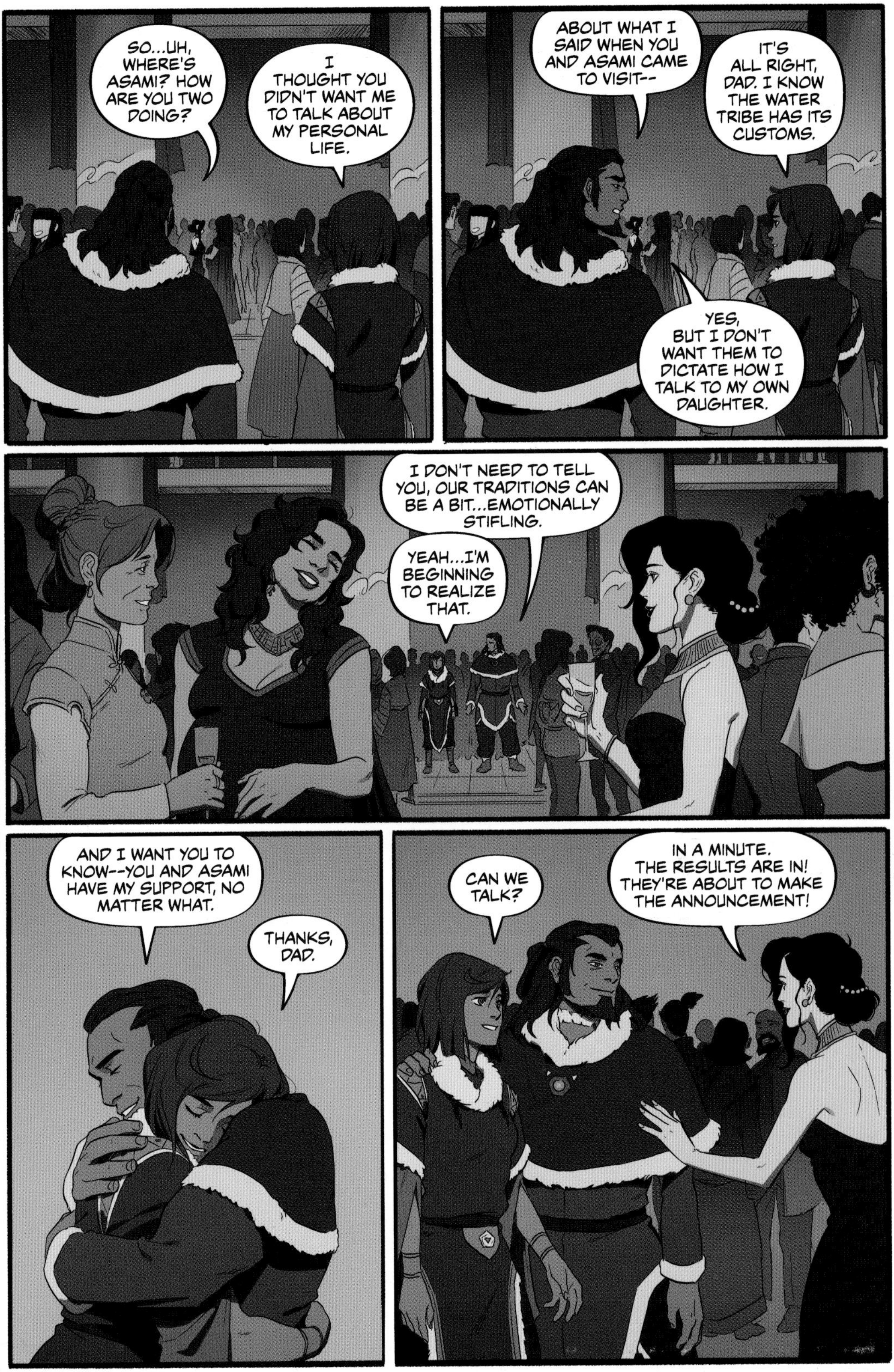
SO...UH, WHERE'S ASAMI? HOW ARE YOU TWO DOING?
I THOUGHT YOU DIDN'T WANT ME TO TALK ABOUT MY PERSONAL LIFE.
ABOUT WHAT I SAID WHEN YOU AND ASAMI CAME TO VISIT--
IT'S ALL RIGHT, DAD. I KNOW THE WATER TRIBE HAS ITS CUSTOMS.
YES, BUT I DON'T WANT THEM TO DICTATE HOW I TALK TO MY OWN DAUGHTER.
I DON'T NEED TO TELL YOU, OUR TRADITIONS CAN BE A BIT...EMOTIONALLY STIFLING.
YEAH...I'M BEGINNING TO REALIZE THAT.
AND I WANT YOU TO KNOW--YOU AND ASAMI HAVE MY SUPPORT, NO MATTER WHAT.
THANKS, DAD.
CAN WE TALK?
IN A MINUTE. THE RESULTS ARE IN! THEY'RE ABOUT TO MAKE THE ANNOUNCEMENT!

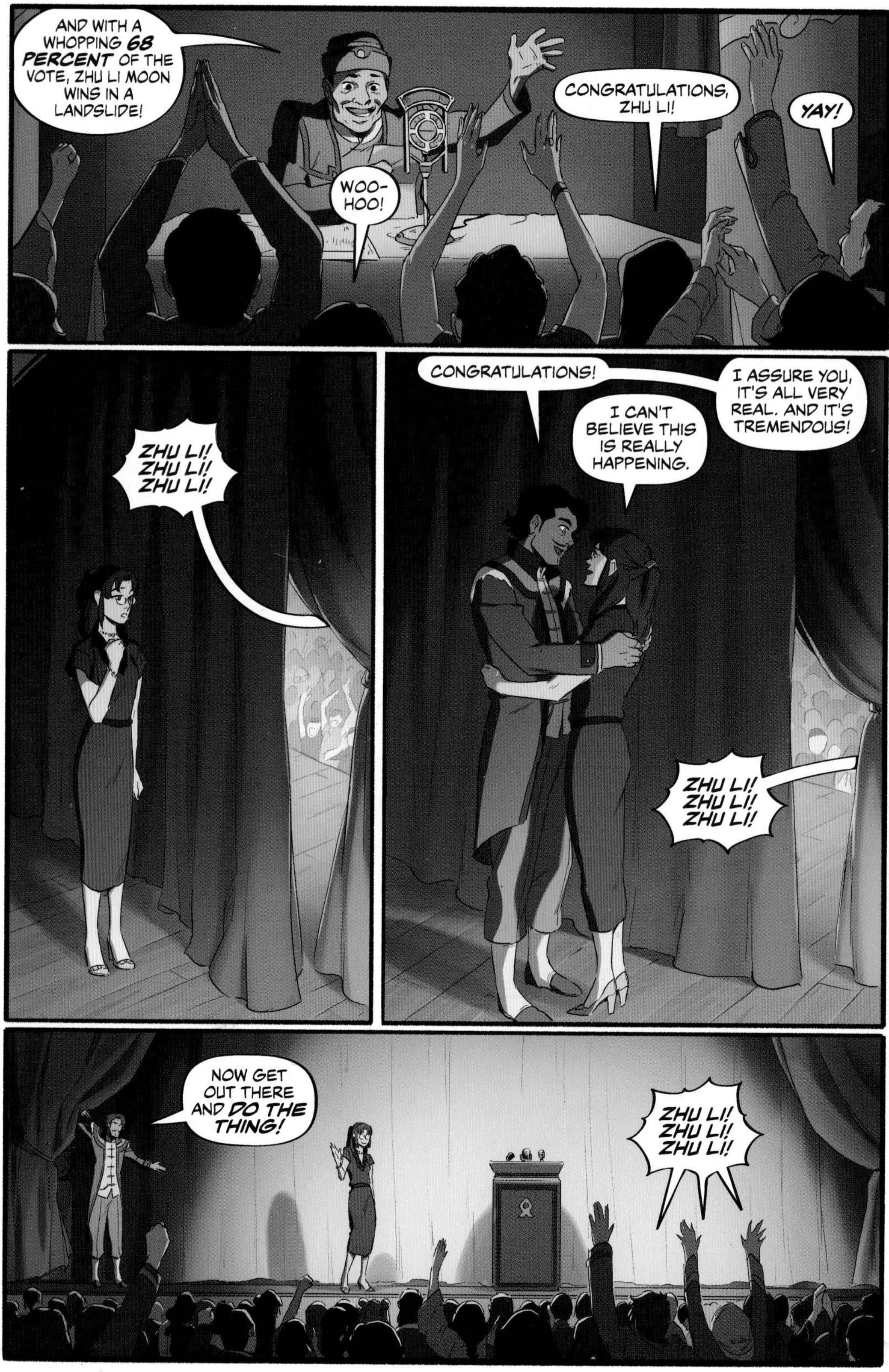
AND WITH A WHOPPING 68 PERCENT OF THE VOTE, ZHU LI MOON WINS IN A LANDSLIDE!
WOO-HOO!
CONGRATULATIONS, ZHU LI!
YAY!
ZHU LI! ZHU LI! ZHU LI!
CONGRATULATIONS!
I CAN'T BELIEVE THIS IS REALLY HAPPENING.
I ASSURE YOU, IT'S ALL VERY REAL. AND IT'S TREMENDOUS!
ZHU LI! ZHU LI! ZHU LI!
NOW GET OUT THERE AND DO THE THING!
ZHU LI! ZHU LI! ZHU LI!

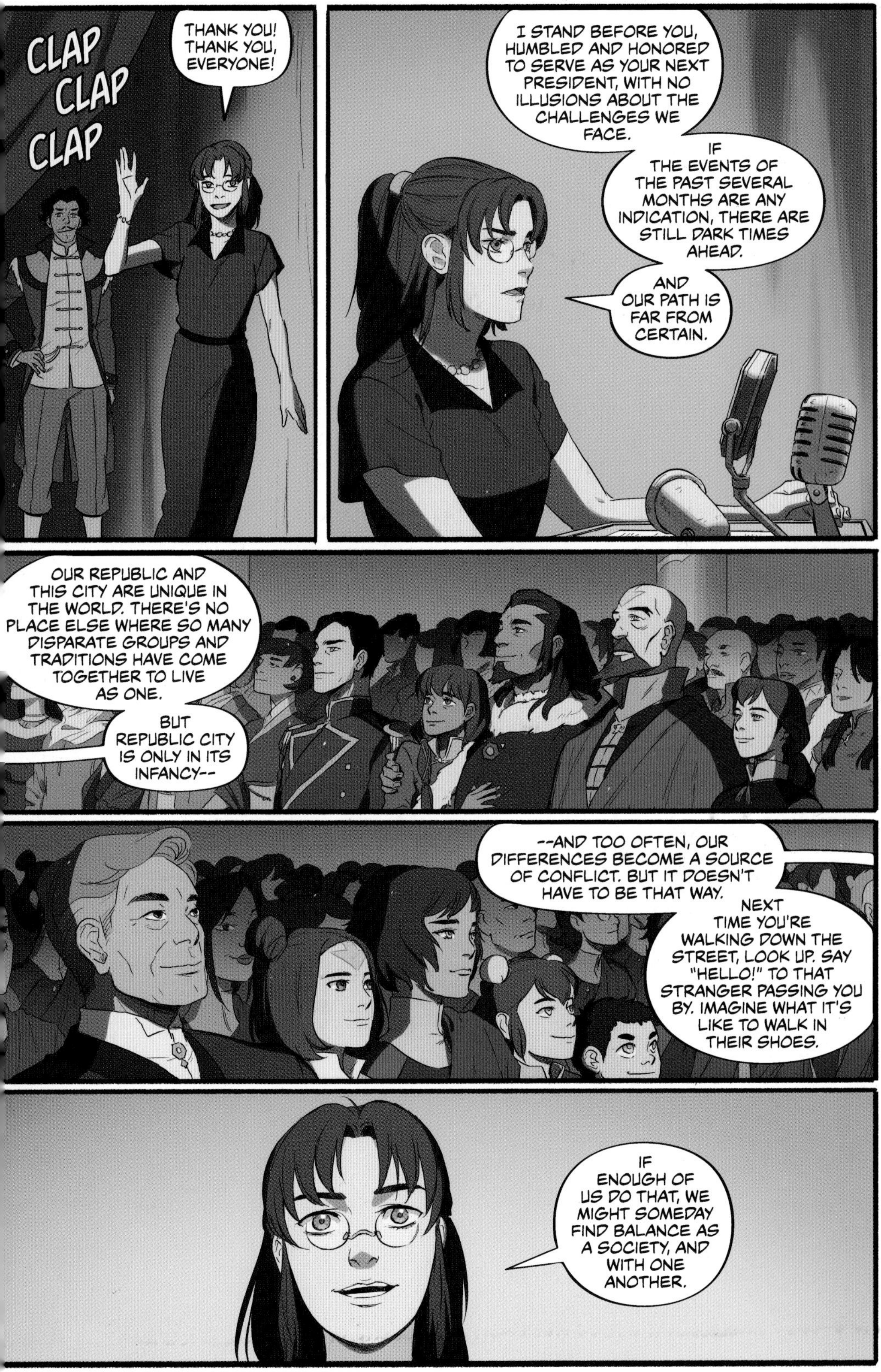
CLAP CLAP CLAP
THANK YOU! THANK YOU, EVERYONE!
I STAND BEFORE YOU, HUMBLED AND HONORED TO SERVE AS YOUR NEXT PRESIDENT, WITH NO ILLUSIONS ABOUT THE CHALLENGES WE FACE.
IF THE EVENTS OF THE PAST SEVERAL MONTHS ARE ANY INDICATION, THERE ARE STILL DARK TIMES AHEAD.
AND OUR PATH IS FAR FROM CERTAIN.
OUR REPUBLIC AND THIS CITY ARE UNIQUE IN THE WORLD. THERE'S NO PLACE ELSE WHERE SO MANY DISPARATE GROUPS AND TRADITIONS HAVE COME TOGETHER TO LIVE AS ONE.
BUT REPUBLIC CITY IS ONLY IN ITS INFANCY--
--AND TOO OFTEN, OUR DIFFERENCES BECOME A SOURCE OF CONFLICT. BUT IT DOESN'T HAVE TO BE THAT WAY.
NEXT TIME YOU'RE WALKING DOWN THE STREET, LOOK UP. SAY "HELLO!" TO THAT STRANGER PASSING YOU BY. IMAGINE WHAT IT'S LIKE TO WALK IN THEIR SHOES.
IF ENOUGH OF US DO THAT, WE MIGHT SOMEDAY FIND BALANCE AS A SOCIETY, AND WITH ONE ANOTHER.

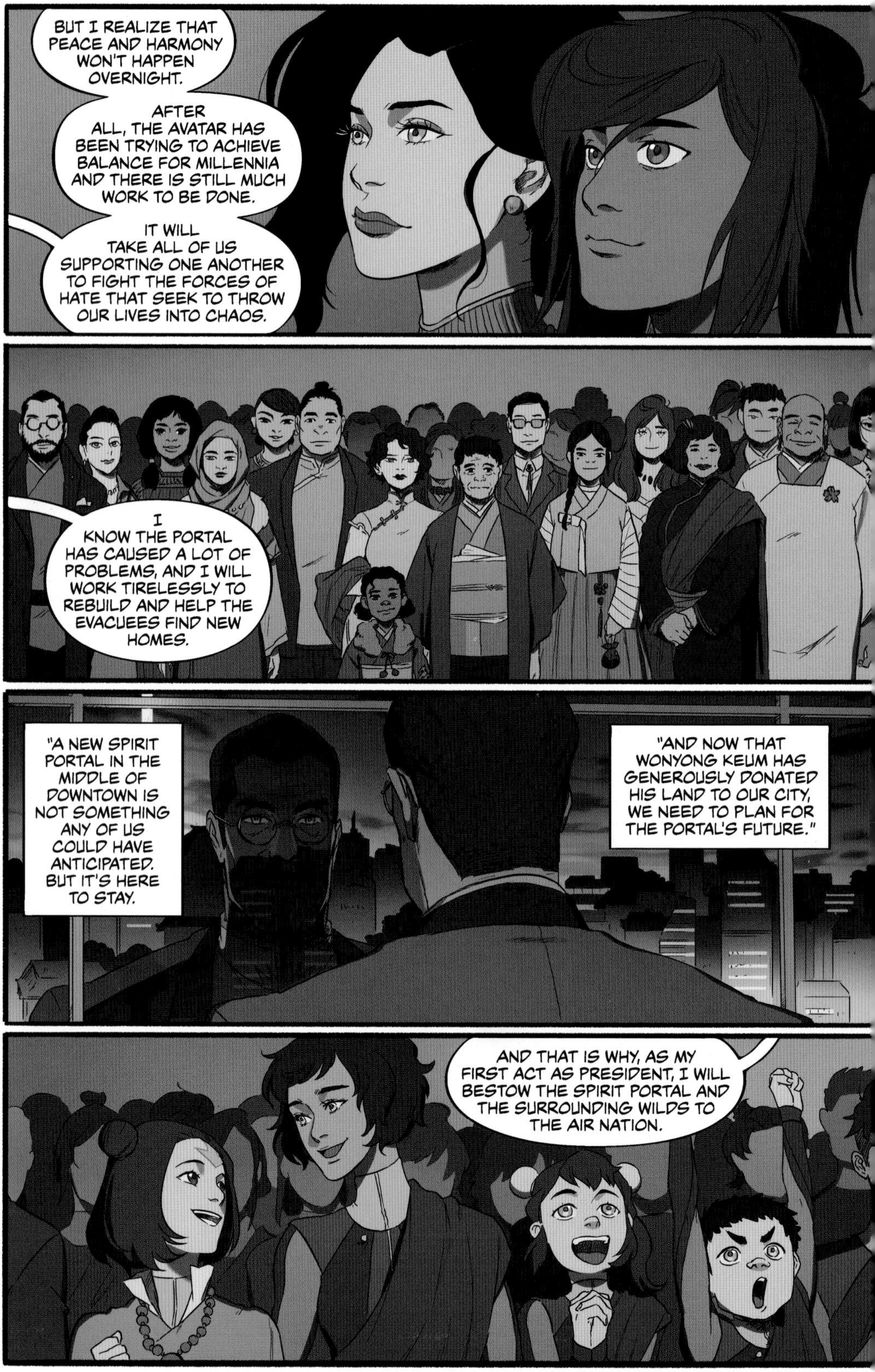
BUT I REALIZE THAT PEACE AND HARMONY WON'T HAPPEN OVERNIGHT.
AFTER ALL, THE AVATAR HAS BEEN TRYING TO ACHIEVE BALANCE FOR MILLENNIA AND THERE IS STILL MUCH WORK TO BE DONE.
IT WILL TAKE ALL OF US SUPPORTING ONE ANOTHER TO FIGHT THE FORCES OF HATE THAT SEEK TO THROW OUR LIVES INTO CHAOS.
I KNOW THE PORTAL HAS CAUSED A LOT OF PROBLEMS, AND I WILL WORK TIRELESSLY TO REBUILD AND HELP THE EVACUEES FIND NEW HOMES.
"A NEW SPIRIT PORTAL IN THE MIDDLE OF DOWNTOWN IS NOT SOMETHING ANY OF US COULD HAVE ANTICIPATED. BUT IT'S HERE TO STAY.
"AND NOW THAT WONYONG KEUM HAS GENEROUSLY DONATED HIS LAND TO OUR CITY, WE NEED TO PLAN FOR THE PORTAL'S FUTURE."
AND THAT IS WHY, AS MY FIRST ACT AS PRESIDENT, I WILL BESTOW THE SPIRIT PORTAL AND THE SURROUNDING WILDS TO THE AIR NATION.

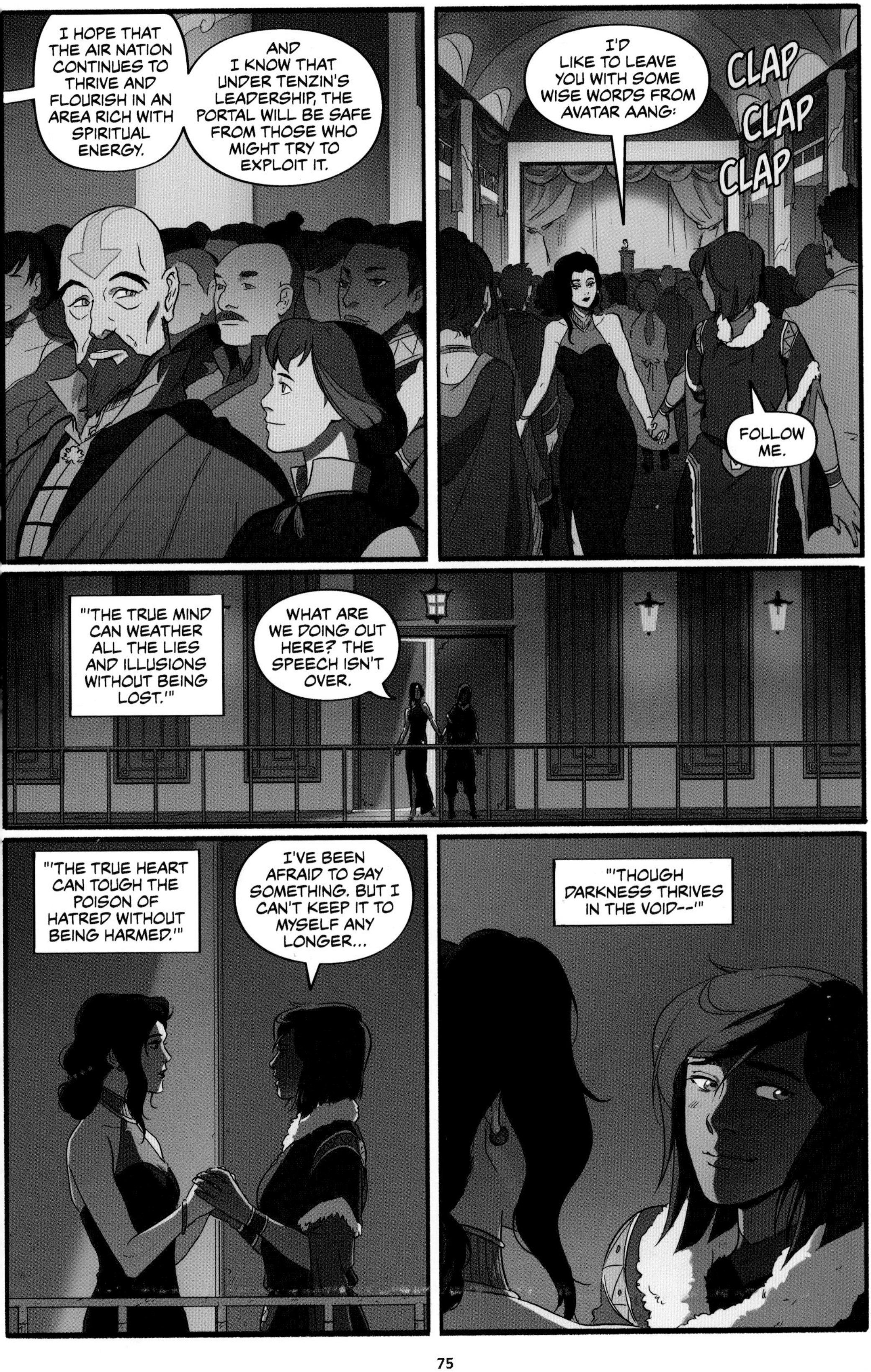
I HOPE THAT THE AIR NATION CONTINUES TO THRIVE AND FLOURISH IN AN AREA RICH WITH SPIRITUAL ENERGY.
AND I KNOW THAT UNDER TENZIN'S LEADERSHIP, THE PORTAL WILL BE SAFE FROM THOSE WHO MIGHT TRY TO EXPLOIT IT.
I'D LIKE TO LEAVE YOU WITH SOME WISE WORDS FROM AVATAR AANG:
CLAP
CLAP
CLAP
FOLLOW ME.
"'THE TRUE MIND CAN WEATHER ALL THE LIES AND ILLUSIONS WITHOUT BEING LOST.'"
WHAT ARE WE DOING OUT HERE? THE SPEECH ISN'T OVER.
"'THE TRUE HEART CAN TOUGH THE POISON OF HATRED WITHOUT BEING HARMED.'"
I'VE BEEN AFRAID TO SAY SOMETHING. BUT I CAN'T KEEP IT TO MYSELF ANY LONGER...
"'THOUGH DARKNESS THRIVES IN THE VOID--'"

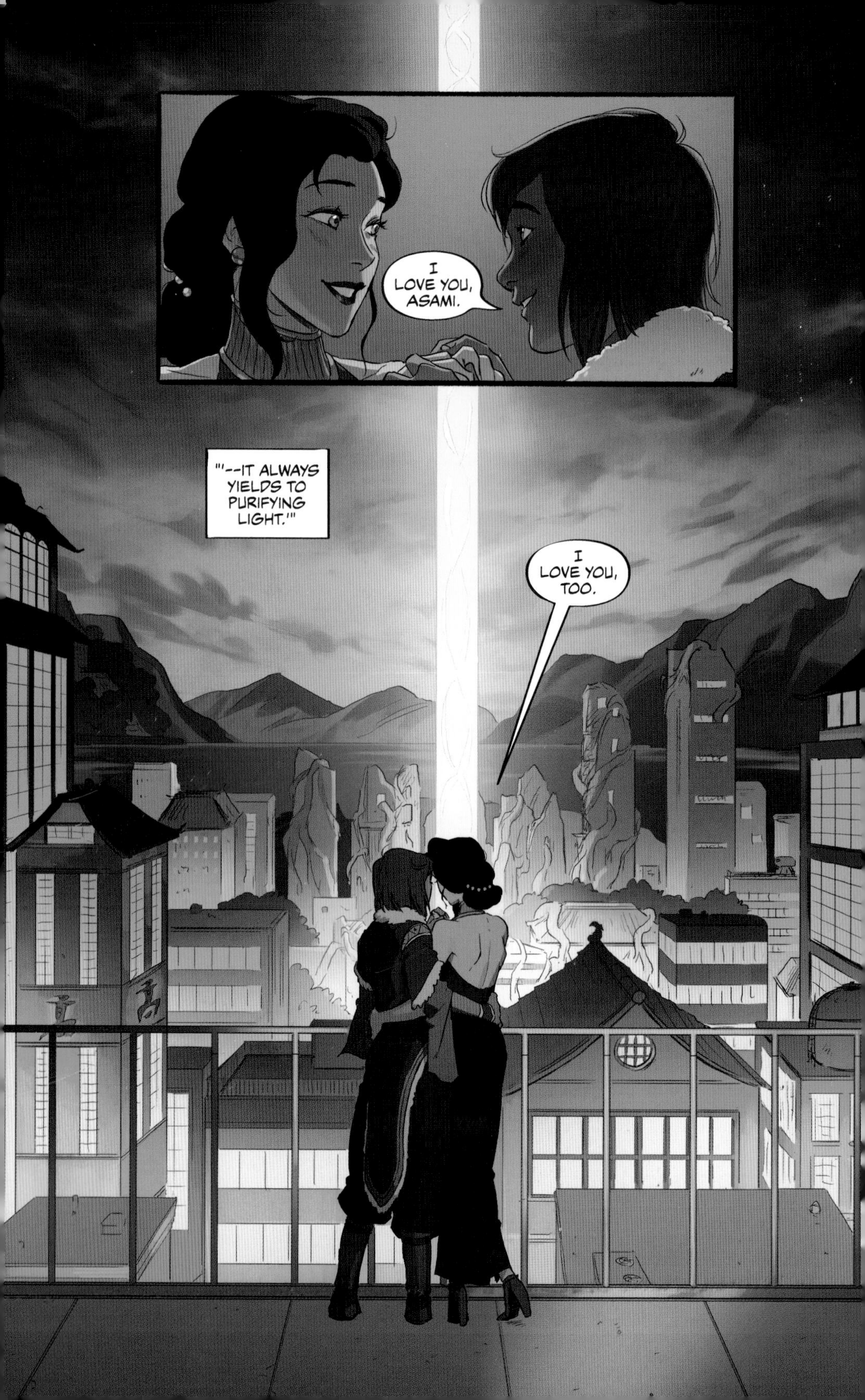
I LOVE YOU, ASAMI.
"'--IT ALWAYS YIELDS TO PURIFYING LIGHT.'"
I LOVE YOU, TOO.

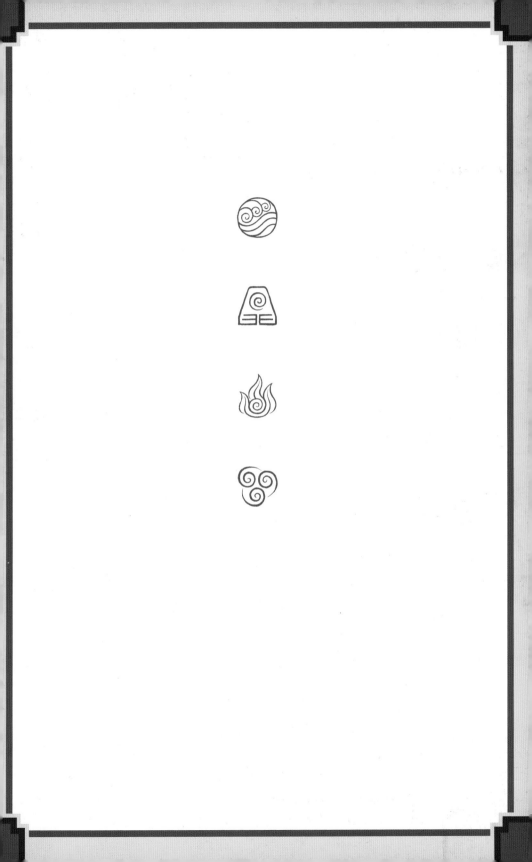

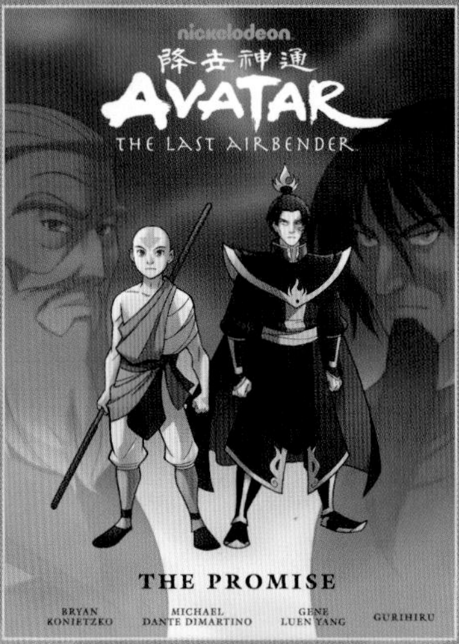
nickelodeon
降世神通
AVATAR
THE LAST AIRBENDER
THE PROMISE
BRYAN KONIETZKO
MICHAEL DANTE DIMARTINO
GENE LUEN YANG
GURIHIRU

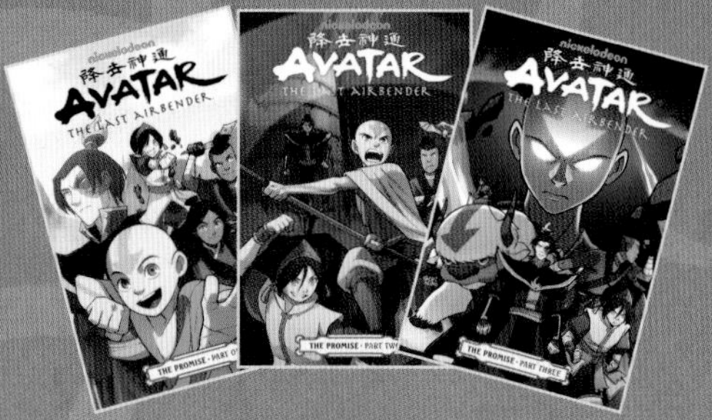
nickelodeon
降世神通
AVATAR
THE LAST AIRBENDER
THE PROMISE · PART TWO
THE PROMISE · PART THREE

Avatar: The Last Airbender—The Promise Library Edition
978-1-61655-074-5 $39.99

Avatar: The Last Airbender—The Promise Part 1
978-1-59582-811-8 $10.99

Avatar: The Last Airbender—The Promise Part 2
978-1-59582-875-0 $10.99

Avatar: The Last Airbender—The Promise Part 3
978-1-59582-941-2 $10.99

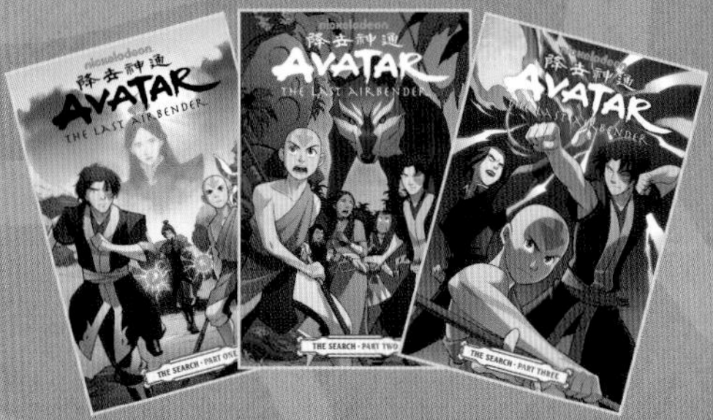
nickelodeon
降世神通
AVATAR
THE LAST AIRBENDER
THE SEARCH · PART ONE
THE SEARCH · PART TWO
THE SEARCH · PART THREE

Avatar: The Last Airbender—The Search Library Edition
978-1-61655-226-8 $39.99

Avatar: The Last Airbender—The Search Part 1
978-1-61655-054-7 $10.99

Avatar: The Last Airbender—The Search Part 2
978-1-61655-190-2 $10.99

Avatar: The Last Airbender—The Search Part 3
978-1-61655-184-1 $10.99

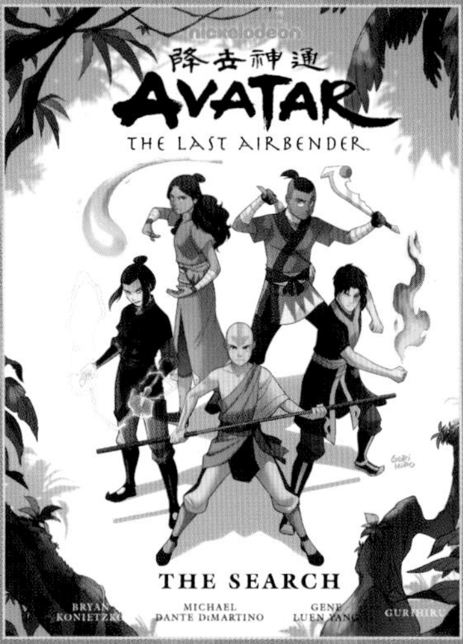
nickelodeon
降世神通
AVATAR
THE LAST AIRBENDER
THE SEARCH
MICHAEL DANTE DiMARTINO
GURIHIRU

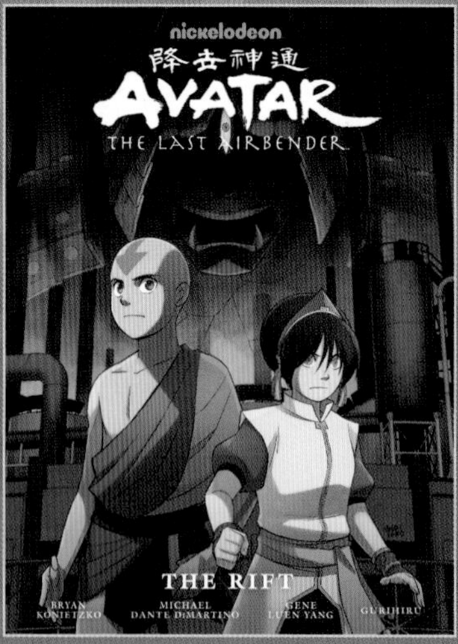
nickelodeon
降世神通
AVATAR
THE LAST AIRBENDER
THE RIFT
BRYAN KONIETZKO
MICHAEL DANTE DiMARTINO
GENE LUEN YANG
GURIHIRU

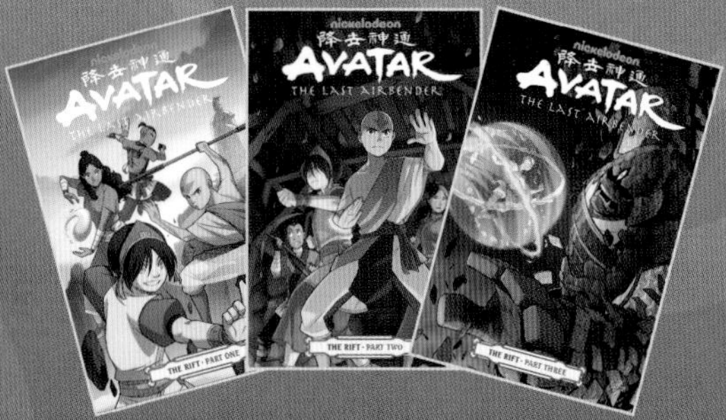
nickelodeon
降世神通
AVATAR
THE LAST AIRBENDER
THE RIFT · PART ONE
THE RIFT · PART TWO
THE RIFT · PART THREE

Avatar: The Last Airbender—The Rift Library Edition
978-1-61655-550-4 $39.99

Avatar: The Last Airbender—The Rift Part 1
978-1-61655-295-4 $10.99

Avatar: The Last Airbender—The Rift Part 2
978-1-61655-296-1 $10.99

Avatar: The Last Airbender—The Rift Part 3
978-1-61655-297-8 $10.99

nickelodeon
降去神通
AVATAR
THE LAST AIRBENDER
SMOKE AND SHADOW

Avatar: The Last Airbender—
Smoke and Shadow Library Edition
978-1-50670-013-7 $39.99

Avatar: The Last Airbender—
Smoke and Shadow Part 1
978-1-61655-761-4 $10.99

Avatar: The Last Airbender—
Smoke and Shadow Part 2
978-1-61655-790-4 $10.99

Avatar: The Last Airbender—
Smoke and Shadow Part 3
978-1-61655-838-3 $10.99

nickelodeon
降去神通
AVATAR
THE LAST AIRBENDER
NORTH AND SOUTH
BRYAN KONIETZKO
MICHAEL DANTE DiMARTINO
GENE LUEN YANG
GURIHIRU

Avatar: The Last Airbender—
North and South Part 1
978-1-50670-022-9 $10.99

Avatar: The Last Airbender—
North and South Part 2
978-1-50670-129-5 $10.99

Avatar: The Last Airbender—
North and South Part 3
978-1-50670-130-1 $10.99

Avatar: The Last Airbender—
North And South Library Edition
978-1-50670-195-0 $39.99

Avatar: The Last Airbender—
The Art of the Animated Series
978-1-59582-504-9 $34.99

Avatar: The Last Airbender—
The Lost Adventures
978-1-59582-748-7 $14.99

nickelodeon
降去神通
AVATAR
THE LAST AIRBENDER

BE PART OF THE INCREDIBLE JOURNEY!

Check out the best-selling graphic novels by acclaimed writer Gene Luen Yang.

AVAILABLE AT YOUR LOCAL COMICS SHOP OR BOOKSTORE.
To find a comics shop in your area, call 1-888-266-4226
For more information or to order direct, visit DarkHorse.com or call 1-800-862-0052

DARK HORSE BOOKS

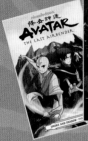

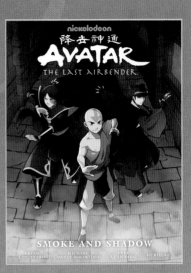

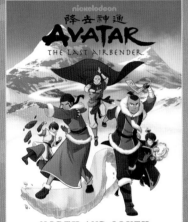

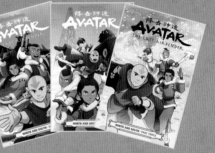

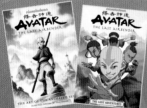

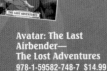

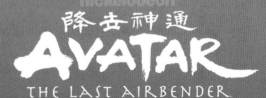

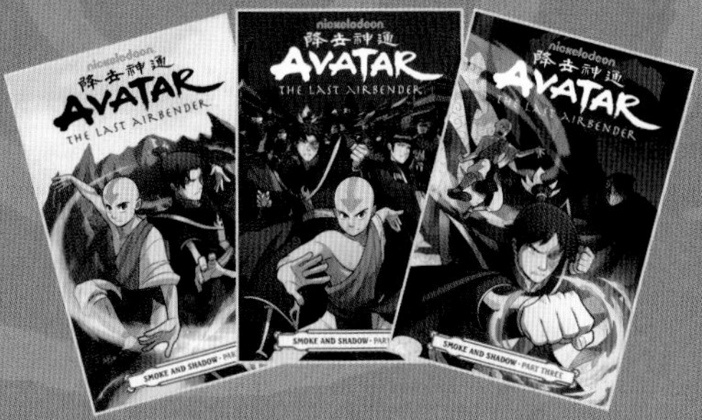

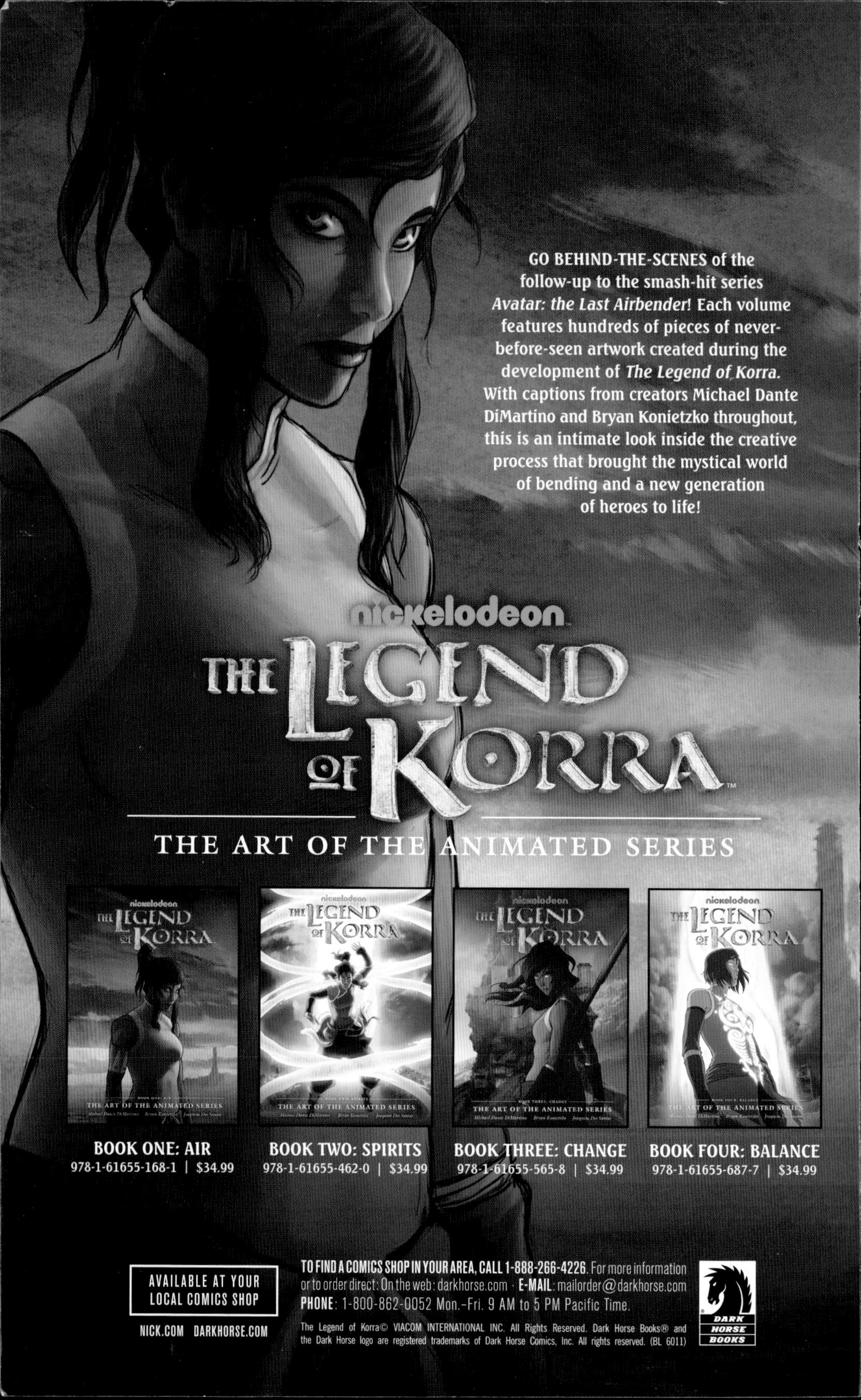
GO BEHIND-THE-SCENES of the follow-up to the smash-hit series *Avatar: the Last Airbender*! Each volume features hundreds of pieces of never-before-seen artwork created during the development of *The Legend of Korra*. With captions from creators Michael Dante DiMartino and Bryan Konietzko throughout, this is an intimate look inside the creative process that brought the mystical world of bending and a new generation of heroes to life!
nickelodeon
THE LEGEND OF KORRA™
THE ART OF THE ANIMATED SERIES
BOOK ONE: AIR
978-1-61655-168-1 | $34.99
BOOK TWO: SPIRITS
978-1-61655-462-0 | $34.99
BOOK THREE: CHANGE
978-1-61655-565-8 | $34.99
BOOK FOUR: BALANCE
978-1-61655-687-7 | $34.99
AVAILABLE AT YOUR LOCAL COMICS SHOP
NICK.COM DARKHORSE.COM
TO FIND A COMICS SHOP IN YOUR AREA, CALL 1-888-266-4226. For more information or to order direct: On the web: darkhorse.com · E-MAIL: mailorder@darkhorse.com
PHONE: 1-800-862-0052 Mon.-Fri. 9 AM to 5 PM Pacific Time.
The Legend of Korra© VIACOM INTERNATIONAL INC. All Rights Reserved. Dark Horse Books® and the Dark Horse logo are registered trademarks of Dark Horse Comics, Inc. All rights reserved. (BL 6011)
DARK HORSE BOOKS